RAND NATIONAL DEFENSE RESEARCH INSTITUTE

T0146381

Analyses of the Department of Defense Acquisition Workforce

Update to Methods and Results through FY 2011

Susan M. Gates, Elizabeth Roth, Sinduja Srinivasan, Lindsay Daugherty

Prepared for the Office of the Secretary of Defense

The research described in this report was prepared for the National Intelligence Council. The research was conducted within the RAND National Defense Research Institute, a federally funded research and development center sponsored by the Office of the Secretary of Defense, the Joint Staff, the Unified Combatant Commands, the Navy, the Marine Corps, the defense agencies, and the defense Intelligence Community under Contract W74V8H-06-C-0002. .

Library of Congress Cataloging-in-Publication Data

Gates, Susan M., 1968-
  Analyses of the Department of Defense acquisition workforce : update to methods and results through FY 2011 / Susan M. Gates, Elizabeth Roth, Sinduja Srinivasan, Lindsay Daugherty.
      p. cm.
  Includes bibliographical references.
  ISBN 978-0-8330-8058-5 (pbk. : alk. paper)
  1. United States. Department of Defense—Procurement—Management. 2. United States. Department of Defense—Personnel management--Evaluation. 3. Civil service—United States—Personnel management. I. Title.

      UC263.G37 2013
      355.6'212—dc23   2013030457

RAND OFFICES
SANTA MONICA, CA • WASHINGTON, DC
PITTSBURGH, PA • NEW ORLEANS, LA • JACKSON, MS • BOSTON, MA
DOHA, QA • CAMBRIDGE, UK • BRUSSELS, BE
www.rand.org

Preface

The defense acquisition workforce (AW), which included over 152,000 military and civilian personnel in FY 2011, is responsible for providing a wide range of acquisition, technology, and logistics support (products and services), to the nation's warfighters. In 2009, the Department of Defense (DoD) initiated a workforce growth initiative for the AW, designed to address concerns about its capacity to achieve its objectives. The objective of this growth initiative was to increase the DoD civilian AW by 20,000 between FYs 2008 and 2015. The Under Secretary of Defense for Acquisition, Technology, and Logistics (USD [AT&L]) has made it a top priority to support DoD human capital strategies and has directed deployment of a comprehensive workforce analysis capability to support enterprisewide and component assessments of the defense acquisition workforce. The Director, AT&L Human Capital Initiatives is responsible for departmentwide strategic human capital management for DoD's AW.

This report provides updates and improvements to the information presented in a previous RAND technical report (Gates et al., 2008). Of particular note, this report describes modifications to the methodology for counting gains, losses, and switches and to our original methodology for projecting inventory. The data sources and original methods are fully described in the previous report.

This report will be of interest to officials responsible for AW planning and management in DoD. This research was sponsored by USD (AT&L) and conducted within the Forces and Resources Policy Center of RAND's National Defense Research Institute, a federally funded research and development center sponsored by the Office of the Secretary of Defense, the Joint Staff, the Unified Combatant Commands, the Department of the Navy, the Marine Corps, the defense agencies, and the defense Intelligence Community. For more information on RAND's Forces and Resources Policy Center, contact the Director, John Winker. He can be reached by email at John_Winkler@rand.org; by phone at 703-413-1100, extension 5511; or by mail at the RAND Corporation, 1200 South Hayes Street, Arlington, VA 22202. More information about RAND is available at http://www.rand.org.

Contents

Figures

Tables

Summary

The defense acquisition workforce (AW) is charged with providing the Department of Defense (DoD) with the management, technical, and business capabilities needed to oversee defense acquisition programs from start to finish. This workforce comprises military personnel, civilian employees of DoD, and contractors who perform functions related to the acquisition of goods and services for DoD.

In 2006, RAND National Defense Research Institute began to collaborate with DoD to develop data-based tools that would support analysis of the organic defense AW, which includes military personnel and DoD civilian employees, but not contractors. RAND published a report in 2008 (Gates et al., 2008) that documented the construction of the data set and the analytical methods used to examine these data. That report provided descriptive analyses of the organic AW based on data through FY 2006.

This report updates Gates et al., 2008, by documenting revisions to the study methods, providing descriptive information on the AW through fiscal year (FY) 2011, and providing a user's manual for a projection model that can help managers explore what shape the AW could take in 2021 under different assumptions about the future. The value of the model and resulting projections is not so much in the specific numbers the model provides (including the examples presented in this report) but in the insights that managers can gain by manipulating the model to examine the possible effects of changes to the model parameters. To illustrate this value, we present some practical examples that describe how a manager can use the model to explore alternative assumptions about future workforce turnover or workforce management practices by modifying some of the default gain and loss rates in the model, which are based on the five-year historical averages. The examples illustrate the implications of such changes for the projections. Appendix A describes the procedures for making such modifications.

At the time of this writing, we continue to work collaboratively with DoD to improve the data and methodologies to make them more useful to DoD AW managers and to update the analyses as new data become available. In addition, we continue to explore new questions with the data we have and are working to obtain additional data, including data on the federalwide AW.

Data

Our analysis uses data on the DoD-wide AW that the Defense Manpower Data Center provided RAND. These data include information on individuals who are classified as part of the AW per DoD Instruction 5000.55. That instruction provides guidance for the implementation of the Defense Acquisition Workforce Improvement Act (DAWIA), which, among other things, required DoD to track the AW. These data are often referred to as *DAWIA data*, and the number of employees captured in the data is referred to as *the DAWIA count*. This is one of several counting methods used since 1992. Congress and DoD raised numerous concerns about the counting methodologies in the 1990, leading to a major effort to improve them in the early 2000s. Because of limitations and changes to the workforce count information, readers are urged to use caution in interpreting trends related to the AW prior to 2004.

Study Approach Was Modified in Five Important Ways

A key objective of this report is to document refinements and improvements that have been incorporated into our analytical approach since the publication of Gates et al., 2008. The following subsections briefly describe the methodology-related modifications.

Better Accounting for Separations and New Hires

In our prior report, we used a "forward looking" approach to define separations in a given fiscal year and a "backward looking" approach to define new hires. Individuals were counted as a separation only if they left the data set and never reappeared. Similarly, individuals were counted as new hires only if they appeared in the data set for the first time ever.

We have modified our definition of separations and new hires so that individuals are considered to be separations in year $t + 1$ if they do appear in the data set in year t but do not appear in year $t + 1$. Similarly, we identify new hires as individuals who do not appear in the data set in year t but do appear in year $t + 1$, even if we observe them in the DoD workforce in a previous year prior to year t. This approach is reflected in all analyses presented in this report.

A key advantage of the new approach is that workforce gains and losses will equal differences in total workforce from year to year. Specifically, the baseline population at the end of year t plus the gains in year $t + 1$ minus the losses in year $t + 1$ will equal the year $t + 1$ population. Separation and new hire rates are slightly higher than they were under the old definition.

Better Coding of Substantive Career Switches to Reflect the Reasons for Pay Plan Changes

In our prior report, we highlighted the fact that a large share of gains and losses to the AW involves individuals who are not gains or losses to the DoD workforce as a whole but who are switching in or out of the AW while remaining DoD employees. We proposed an approach for distinguishing between switches that seemed to be substantive and those that appeared to have been purely administrative. Using this approach, switches were coded as either *substantive* or *administrative*. Coding was based on whether one or more of the following fields in an individual's personnel record changed in conjunction with the switch between AW and non-AW: agency, bureau, functional occupational group, occupational series, or pay plan.

Between 2006 and 2011, however, numerous DoD employees experienced pay plan changes that were completely administrative because of the implementation and retraction of the National Security Personnel System. After exploring this issue in depth, we have modified the definition of a *substantive* switch so that pay plan is no longer a trigger unless one of the pay plans involved is the Senior Executive Service and to include pay grade as a trigger when the pay plan has not changed.

More Accurate Accounting for Retirement Eligibility

The vast majority of civil servants DoD currently employs participate in one of two retirement plans: the Civil Service Retirement System (CSRS) and the Federal Employees Retirement System (FERS).[1] FERS was created in 1986; anyone hired into the federal civil service after January 1, 1987, is automatically covered under FERS. Employees hired prior to that date were covered by CSRS when they were hired but had the option to switch into FERS.

For the purposes of this analysis, we created a variable for each individual covered under either CSRS or FERS called "years relative to retirement eligibility." We did this by calculating the earliest age at which each individual could claim regular, full retirement benefits given their current retirement plan, age, and years of service under the assumption that they work continuously until that future retirement eligibility date and remain covered under their current retirement plan. In our previous report, we calculated this based on year-of-birth information. In this report, we make use of data on month and year of birth, which more accurately indicate retirement eligibility.

Accounting for Differences in Observations Presented by Data

By linking records across data files, we are now able to perform analyses that were not possible in analyses of cross-sectional data. The process of linking data from multiple sources also uncovered some inconsistencies across files that required us to either drop records from the analysis or reclassify records.

Update of Projection Model for Accuracy and Utility

The original projection model used five-year historical average gain and loss rates for a population to project workforce size over the next ten years, assuming that historical averages would continue into the future. The new version of the projection model differs from the prior version in two important respects. First, the model is now based on years relative to retirement eligibility, rather than years of service. Second, we added a component to the projection model worksheet that allows the user to input a target workforce size each year for the next ten years. The model then generates a projection of the number of new hires necessary to achieve, or at least come near, that goal. Finally, we have applied the projection model not only to the AW as a whole but also to subsets of the AW.

Revised Methods and Updated Data Elicited a Number of Important Findings

Here, we present a brief descriptive overview of the AW based on current methods and data. We also offer a projection of the AW in 2012, assuming current hiring and attrition trends hold constant.

The Acquisition Growth Initiative Was Associated with Growth in AW

Consistent with the AW growth initiative the Secretary of Defense established in April 2009, we found that the AW grew by 22 percent between FY 2008 and FY 2011. Along with new hiring, gains occurred through internal transfers into the AW ("switches in"). Similarly, losses occurred that were due to exits from DoD or to internal transfers out of the AW ("switches

---

[1] In FY 2011, 662 out of 136,066 civilian AW employees were covered by retirement plans other than CSRS or FERS.

out"). The number of new hires into the AW, as well as hiring rates, increased dramatically in FY 2008 and remained high through FY 2011.

Military AW Representation Is Highest in Air Force

Historically, the military AW has been smaller than the civilian AW. Figure S.1 displays civilian and military totals by service as of September 2011. Notably, military personnel are most prominent in the Air Force's AW.

AW Attrition Remained Low

AW attrition, defined in terms of the percentage of the AW that leaves DoD civilian employment in a given year, has been consistently lower than DoD civilian norms, largely due to lower voluntary and involuntary separations. Notably, for both the AW and the overall civilian workforce, the rate of exit declined slightly in FY 2008, more significantly in FY 2009, remained low in FY 2010, and increased in FY 2011. FYs 2009 and 2010 saw unusually low rates of voluntary separation and retirement, likely because of high unemployment rates and concerns about stock market and pension valuations.

Gain and Loss Patterns Vary Across Subpopulations of the Workforce

An important example of these differences is among science technology engineering and mathematics (STEM) personnel. When compared with personnel fields across DoD, the overlap between the AW and STEM populations is substantial. Approximately 25 percent of the DoD civilian workforce is in either STEM fields or the AW; 17 percent is AW, and 15 percent is STEM. Seven percent are both STEM and AW, and another 8 percent are STEM but not AW. Our comparison of workforce numbers suggested that the AW STEM workforce has consistently higher retention than either the overall AW population or the DoD-wide STEM population.

Figure S.1
Total Civilian and Military Acquisition Workers, by Service, 2011

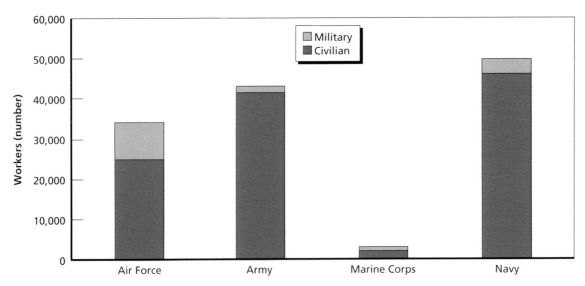

The Projection Model Can Be Used to Explore Expected Future Growth Patterns Under Different Scenarios

The value of the workforce projection model described in this report lies in its flexibility, which allows managers to explore alternative scenarios. Recent data on hiring and attrition were used to produce workforce projections to 2021 if recent gain and loss rates were to continue into the future. In presenting this information, we are not suggesting that past trends *will* continue and this *will* be the future size of the workforce. That said, these projections can provide a useful starting point for workforce managers. The baseline workforce size used for the projection models is 135,320 (FY 2011). Between FY 2006 and FY 2011, the average hiring rate was 8 percent, and the attrition rate was 5.2 percent. Figure S.2 suggests that, if historical gain and separation rates hold over the next decade, the civilian AW will grow substantially over the next ten years, reaching over 213,132 by 2021.[2] The model has flexibilities that allow managers to explore scenarios other than those suggested by relatively high recent averages. For example, recognizing that further growth of the AW is impossible, given the available resources and the end of the AW growth initiative, we also generated projections for two alternative scenarios that align more closely with long-term historical averages. A new hire rate of 3 percent per year leads to a projected *decline* of the AW to 126,355 by FY 2021. An assumed hiring rate of 4 percent per year leads to a prediction of slight workforce growth to 140,909 by FY 2021. An alternative version of the model allows users to input target end strengths for future fiscal years and see the number of new hires required to achieve the targets. Appendix A describes how managers can manipulate the model.

Figure S.2
Projections of the Size of the DoD Civilian Acquisition Workforce, FY 2011–2021

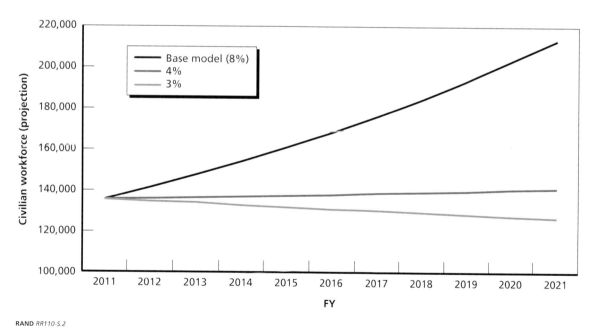

RAND *RR110-S.2*

---

[2]   The projected future size of the AW is also influenced by gains and losses to the AW due to internal transfers from within DoD. Because internal gains into the AW from other parts of DoD typically exceed internal losses, the projection will be stable, even though the rate of external hiring is lower than the expected rate of attrition.

Conclusions and Recommendations

This report describes some of the workforce supply analyses of the DoD AW that DoD data can support. Supply analysis is only part of the strategic human capital planning. Supply analyses must ultimately be combined with demand analyses. As defense budgets come under pressure, DoD must ensure that the civilian workforce is structured as efficiently as possible. A more-systematic and data-based understanding of workload drivers for the AW and the relationship between changes in the acquisition process and workload levels would facilitate strategic human capital planning for the AW.

One objective of the AW growth initiative was to increase the size of the organic civilian AW through a combination of insourcing contractor positions and new hiring. As we noted in our 2008 report, DoD-wide information on contractors who are performing acquisition-related functions is lacking. To date, there has been little progress in terms of the development of such data. As a result, we were unable to assess the extent to which insourcing contributed to AW growth. Better information on the contract workforce is critical for managers interested in assessing the health of the AW.

Acknowledgments

This work updates an earlier RAND report (Gates et al., 2008). The authors of this report would like to acknowledge the contributions of Edward Keating, Adria Jewell, Lindsay Daugherty, Ralph Masi, Bryan Tysinger, and Albert Robbert, who contributed to that original report. Martha Timmer provided programming support for analyses used in this report.

We are indebted to Garry Shafovaloff for his ongoing support of and contributions to this work. His careful review and use of our ongoing analyses and insightful questions have promoted continuous improvements to our analyses. His comments on an earlier draft improved the clarity and accuracy of the final report. We have benefited from the comments and questions of a number of users of these analyses, notably Jonathan Metts, John Knox, Carolyn Willis, and Michelle LeBlanc. We are grateful to the file managers at the Defense Manpower Data Center who have provided us with data over the years and answered our many questions about the data files: Portia Sullivan, Leslie Nixon, Michael Kolkowski, Peter Cerussi, and Scott Seggerman.

Ray Conley, Chaitra Hardison, and Doug Thompson provided careful reviews of a prior draft. Their comments improved the quality of this final document. We thank Kate Giglio for her efforts to improve the quality of presentation in the document. We thank Donna White for her assistance in formatting and compiling the draft and Phyllis Gilmore for editing the final copy.

The authors alone are responsible for any remaining errors in the document.

Abbreviations

AT&L	Acquisition, Technology, and Logistics
AW	acquisition workforce
CSRS	Civil Service Retirement System
DAWIA	Defense Acquisition Workforce Improvement Act
DCMA	Defense Contract Management Agency
DLA	Defense Logistics Agency
DMDC	Defense Manpower Data Center
DoD	Department of Defense
DoDI	DoD instruction
FERS	Federal Employees Retirement System
FY	fiscal year
GAO	Government Accountability Office
GS	General Schedule
MDA	Missile Defense Agency
MDAP	major defense acquisition programs
MRA	minimum retirement age
NDAA	National Defense Authorization Act
NSPS	National Security Personnel System
OPM	Office of Personnel Management
SES	Senior Executive Service
SPRDE	Systems Planning, Research Development, and Engineering
STEM	Science, Technology, Engineering, and Mathematics
USD (AT&L)	Under Secretary of Defense for Acquisition, Technology, and Logistics

WEX	work experience
YORE	years relative to retirement eligibility
YOS	years of service

CHAPTER ONE

Introduction

The defense acquisition workforce (AW) comprises military personnel, civilian employees of the Department of Defense (DoD), and contractors who perform functions that are related to the acquisition of goods and services for DoD. In 2006, RAND National Defense Research Institute began a collaboration with DoD to develop data-based tools to support analysis of the organic defense AW, which includes military and DoD civilians but not contractors. RAND published a report in 2008 that documented the construction of the data set and the analytical methods used to examine these data (Gates et al., 2008). The report also provided descriptive analyses of the organic AW based on data through fiscal year (FY) 2006. Each year, RAND generates updated summary information on AW gains and losses, for the AW as a whole and for subpopulations of the AW based on the methods described in the 2008 report. Over time, we refine and improve upon the methods to address new challenges and opportunities. The current report updates the earlier document.

The Acquisition Workforce Is Responsible for All Aspects of the Department of Defense Acquisition Process

In response to the Defense Acquisition Workforce Improvement Act (DAWIA) of 1990, DoD has been tracking and reporting on the AW since 1992. The AW is responsible for planning, design, development, testing, contracting, production, introduction, acquisition logistics support, and disposal of systems, equipment, facilities, supplies, or services that are intended for use in, or support of, military missions. A key role of the AW is to provide oversight of the acquisition process. Military and DoD civilian personnel are flagged as part of the AW based on whether they fulfill one or more of these roles. Members of the AW can be found in many different organizations across DoD.

Members of the AW are grouped into career fields. The number and titles of these career fields have changed over time. In FY 2011, there were 13 main career fields:

- auditing
- business, cost estimating, and financial management[1]
- contracting
- facilities engineering
- industrial property management

---

[1] This career field comprises the cost estimating and financial management career paths.

- communications and information technology
- life-cycle logistics
- quality assurance
- program management oversight and program management
- purchasing and procurement
- science and technology
- systems planning, research, development, and engineering (SPRDE)[2]
- test and evaluation engineering.

Recent Challenges Include Conflicting Growth and Budgetary Demands

Our prior report was based on data through the end of FY 2006 and was published in 2008. Since that time, there have been important changes in DoD related to the management of the AW and the overall DoD civilian workforce. In April 2009, the Secretary of Defense announced a major defense AW growth initiative designed to increase the size of the civilian workforce by 20,000 between FYs 2008 and 2015. One-half of the planned growth would come from new hiring, and one-half from insourcing of contractor functions (DoD, 2010). The defense AW growth initiative responded to concerns that the size of the workforce was insufficient to meet DoD procurement demands, particularly if involved in major defense acquisition programs and contingency operations, and that DoD was using contractors to support core acquisition functions.[3] The growth initiative involved a strategic shaping effort that prioritized career fields, such as contracting and SPRDE, that are viewed as critical to improving acquisition outcomes (DoD, 2010, p. 1-5). Section 852 of the 2008 National Defense Authorization Act, Public Law 110-181, established the Defense Acquisition Workforce Development Fund, which provided funds to support recruitment and hiring of acquisition personnel.

Three years into the growth initiative, pressure to reduce DoD budgets and federal spending resulted in efforts to reevaluate workforce requirements (size), taking into consideration changes since 2008. In March 2011, DoD announced a freeze on the number of civilian workers, although an exception was made for recruitment and hiring supported by the Defense Acquisition Workforce Development Fund. The Marine Corps announced a 90-day civilian hiring freeze in December 2010, which was extended until January 2012, when it was replaced by a manage-to-payroll approach. This freeze encompassed the Marine Corps AW (Losey, 2010). The Air Force announced a 90-day civilian hiring freeze effective August 9, 2011, along with plans for strategic use of voluntary separation and retirement incentives. The Army announced plans to cut nearly 9,000 civilian jobs by October 2012 (Clark, 2011a; Clark, 2011b). Although the services have remained committed to the AW rebuilding efforts, it has yet to be determined how these broader pressures on defense budgets and the size of the civilian defense workforce will influence DoD's AW. GAO has urged DoD to align efforts sup-

---

[2]   The SPRDE workforce currently comprises two separate career fields: SPRDE–Systems Engineering, and SPRDE–Program Systems Engineer. The former career field is roughly 100 times larger than the latter one. In our analysis, we combine these two career fields into a single SPRDE career field.

[3]   The U.S. Government Accountability Office (GAO) designated defense contract management and defense weapon system acquisitions as "high risk" (GAO, 2008b). The report of the Acquisition Advisory Panel (2007) criticized government acquisition efforts for excessive use of noncompetitive approaches, and the Gansler Commission Report concluded that major changes were needed in acquisition functions that support expeditionary operations.

ported by the Defense Acquisition Workforce Development Fund with the overall AW plan and to develop outcome-oriented metrics for evaluating the effectiveness of the fund's efforts (GAO, 2012).

At the time of this writing, we continue to work collaboratively with DoD to improve the data and methodologies to make them more useful to DoD AW managers and to update the analyses as new data become available. In addition, we continue to explore new questions with the data we have and are working to obtain additional data, including data on the AW from across the federal government.

Data and Methods

As Gates et al., 2008, describes, RAND has assembled a comprehensive data file that can support a DoD-wide analysis of DoD AW. The RAND data file comprises information drawn from several files that the Defense Manpower Data Center (DMDC) maintains:

- **DoD civilian personnel inventory file:** This file provides annual "snapshots" of each civilian employee, including his or her grade, location, and education level, as well as other demographic variables, as of September 30. The data from this file also include information on an individual's occupation, organization, pay plan, and years of service (YOS).
- **DoD civilian personnel transaction file:** The data from this file complement the inventory data by noting "transactions" for workers between inventory snapshots. The transactions of central interest to us were indicators of attrition, e.g., retirement, voluntary separation, and involuntary separation, as well as codes indicating whether an individual transferred to or from another federal government agency. We obtained civilian inventory and transaction data going back to FY 1980 for this work.
- **Military work experience file (WEX):** The WEX file contains information on anyone who has served in the U.S. military since 1975. This information includes rank, military service, active duty status, and occupation. We use these data not only to characterize the military AW but also to study the extent to which DoD civilian employees have prior military experience and the nature of that experience.
- **Acquisition workforce person file (DoD Instruction [DoDI] 5000.55 submission data) and the AW position file:** These files provide information on the individuals who are designated as part of the AW since FY 1992, as well as on the positions that DoD has designated as acquisition positions. The person file contains a record for each individual (both military and civilian) who was included in the service or agency submissions made in accordance with DoDI 5000.55. Each AW person record includes an AW position code and can thus be linked to the position data.

In the DMDC database, records can be linked across files in useful ways. For example, connections can be made between the military and civilian files or between the civilian inventory file and the acquisition person file. Moreover, searching across time is possible because of a unique identifier (a scrambled social security number) that is used consistently across files and years for a given individual.

Together, the DMDC files contain information on personnel, including their positions, assignments, ranks, pay, occupations, YOS, demographic characteristics, education, acquisition career fields, and acquisition certification level. By linking records across time and across files, we were able to examine movement into and out of the AW, movement between the DoD military and civilian workforces, and promotion and experience trajectories.

The AW Count

As previously mentioned, our analysis uses data on DoD-wide AW the DMDC provided RAND that include information on individuals who are classified as part of the AW per DoDI 5000.55. That instruction provides guidance for the implementation of DAWIA, which among other things required DoD to track its AW. These data are often referred to as *DAWIA data*, and the number of employees the data capture is the *DAWIA count*.

Data on the DAWIA workforce are available from 1992 to the present in a way that allows us to link with other personnel information DoD maintains. For this reason, they are useful for analytical purposes. However, other methods for counting the AW have been used over time. The Packard Commission established a counting methodology, called the *acquisition organization workforce approach*, that counts all personnel employed by the 22 DoD acquisition organizations, regardless of occupation (DoD, Office of the Inspector General, 2006). The refined Packard counting system is a revision of the acquisition organization counting system that excludes some personnel who would not be expected to be involved in acquisition support functions (e.g., human resources personnel or administrative assistants). (Defense Acquisition Structures and Capabilities Review, 2007). The Packard and refined Packard workforce counts tended to be higher than the DAWIA counts because they include individuals who are not actually performing acquisition functions.

DoD reported results of both of these counting methodologies to Congress annually until FY 2004. Beginning with FY 2005, after extensive efforts to review and validate the way in which members of the AW are identified and counted, the DAWIA count has replaced the refined Packard count. DoD Inspector General has concluded that counts from FY 2004 and earlier are not verifiable (see DoD, Office of the Inspector General, 2006). These efforts to revise the definition of the AW resulted in a large number of recategorizations into and out of the AW in the early 2000s, as we described in Gates et al., 2008.

Because of these limitations to the workforce count information, readers are urged to use caution in interpreting trends related to the AW prior to 2004.

Purpose

The purpose of this report is threefold. First, we document modifications and new approaches to the analysis that we have adopted since the publication of Gates et al., 2008. Second, we present updated descriptive information on the AW, applying these new methods to the most recent available data. This descriptive information provides an overview of how the factors described in this introduction, especially the AW growth initiative, have influenced the defense AW. Third, we describe how managers can use these tools and methods to explore workforce projections for the entire workforce or for subsets of the DoD AW (e.g., specific career fields or agencies) under different scenarios, thereby identifying workforce segments that may be in need of some policy intervention.

Outline of Report

The broader policy motivation for this workforce analysis is presented in full in Gates et al., 2008. In Chapter Two, we describe modifications to the analytical methods described in Gates et al., 2008. In Chapter Three, we present an updated overview of the civilian AW using data through FY 2011. Chapter Four provides workforce projections for the civilian AW for key subsets of the AW. Chapter Five presents an overview of the military AW, again using data through FY 2011. Chapter Six concludes. Appendix A provides an updated users' manual for the projection models and technical detail on the updated models. Appendix B summarizes AW gains and losses.

CHAPTER TWO

Overview of Changes to RAND's Workforce Analysis Methodology

Gates et al., 2008, fully describes our data sources and original methods. For the sake of brevity, we review only the data sources in this chapter and provide greater detail on the changes made in our data definitions, analytical approach, and models. We have made a number of improvements in these areas since the earlier report. These changes came about through the process of working with the data and from interacting with DoD on policy-related questions specific to the AW.

Leave and Entrance Patterns Are More Clearly Represented

The analyses we present in this report are descriptive. Unless otherwise noted, the descriptive information on the civilian AW and all DoD civilians includes all appropriated-fund civil service employees. The projections include all civilians who participate in the Civil Service Retirement System (CSRS) and Federal Employees Retirement System (FERS); individuals in other pay plans are excluded. We did not exclude civilians from the analysis based on their pay plan or because they were employed part time. Our analysis of military personnel includes active-duty military members, including activated reservists.[1]

In our prior report, we used a "forward looking" approach to define separations in a given FY and a "backward looking" approach to define new hires (see Gates et al., 2008, p. 9). Individuals were counted as separations only if they left the data set and never reappeared. Similarly, individuals were counted as new hires only if they appeared in the data set for the first time ever.

In conjunction with the Office of the Under Secretary of Defense for Acquisition, Technology and Logistics (AT&L), Human Capital Initiatives, we determined that it was more useful and appropriate to account for all gains and losses in the year that they occur and not exclude reentrants from the separation and new hire calculations. This decision was motivated in part by the fact that, while it is impossible to know whether an employee who separates at a certain time will reenter the workforce in the future, it is possible to look back over nearly 30 years to see whether a new hire has ever before been a member of the workforce.

---

[1] We tracked the military experience of nonactivated reservists but did not include them in the military workforce count. Many of these reservists are currently serving as DoD civilian employees. Future work will strive to better understand the role of nonactivated reservists in the AW.

We therefore modified our definitions of separations and new hires so that individuals are now considered to be new hires in year $t + 1$ if they do not appear in the data set for year t but do appear in that for year $t + 1$, even if we observe them in the DoD workforce in a year previous to year t. Similarly, we now count as separations all losses of individuals who appear in the data set in year t but do not appear in year $t + 1$, even if they return in subsequent years. This approach is reflected in all analyses presented in this report.

The major difference between the two approaches is in accounting for reentrants to the workforce (i.e., people who return to the DoD civilian workforce after some break in service). Reentrants are now treated as separations in the year they leave and as new hires in the year they reenter. This implies that, in a given year, the baseline population at the end of year t plus the gains in year $t + 1$ minus the losses in year $t + 1$ will equal the year $t + 1$ population. Under the new approach, separation and new hire rates are slightly higher than they were under the old definition. In addition, there are changes in the distribution of new hire characteristics—especially in terms of age and prior experience—because reentrants are now included in the new hire group. In the projection models, we are able to account for the characteristics of new hires in terms of prior YOS or years relative to retirement eligibility. We can address questions regarding the behavior of reentrants more directly, as desired by the client, through targeted analyses of this population.

Civilian Substantive Career Switches Are Coded to Better Reflect the Reasons for Pay Plan and Pay Grade Changes

Our prior report highlighted the fact that a large share of gains to and losses from the DoD civilian AW involves individuals who are not gains to and losses from the DoD civilian workforce as a whole but who are switching into or out of the civilian AW while remaining civilian DoD employees.[2]

A concern for policymakers is identifying which of these switches are due to meaningful changes in the nature of work that a person is doing when switching into or out of the AW and which of these switches simply reflect a shift in the perspective of a particular organization as to whether a position (and hence the person filling that position) is coded as part of the AW or not.

In the previous report, we proposed a definition to distinguish between switches that seemed to be substantive and those that appeared to have been purely administrative (see Gates et al., 2008, p. 9), then coded switches accordingly (see Figure 2.1). The original definition, which we call *definition 1* here, is based on whether one or more of the following fields in an individual's personnel record changed in conjunction with the switch between AW and non-AW: agency (e.g., military service), bureau (e.g., major command within a military service), functional occupational group, occupational series, or pay plan. We refer to these fields as *triggers* for classifying a switch as substantive rather than administrative. If one or more of the triggers changed concurrently with the switch into or out of the AW, the switch is classified as substantive; otherwise, it is classified as administrative.

---

[2] Individuals who move from the military AW to the civilian AW are considered to be new hires into the DoD civilian AW, although we can conduct separate analyses of these individuals as needed.

Figure 2.1
Original Definition of Substantive and Administrative Switching Into and Out of the Acquisition Workforce

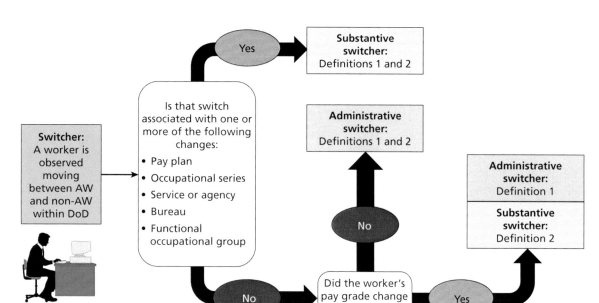

Definition 1: Change in grade level within a pay plan is not a trigger for categorizing a switch as substantive.
Definition 2: Change in grade level within a pay plan is a trigger for categorizing a switch as substantive.
RAND *RR110-2.1*

By distinguishing between these two types of switches, our analysis provided DoD with new insights into the nature of AW gains and losses. These insights are crucial to understanding the relationship between the measured workforce size and workforce capacity. Importantly, increases or decreases in the measured workforce count that are due to administrative gains or losses do not imply an increase or decrease in the size or capacity of the AW. We have been working to refine this definition since 2008.

One question that has been raised about the list of triggers is whether promotions, or changes in pay grade within a pay plan, should be included. After considering this question, we decided to expand the definition of substantive switches to include those that occur in conjunction with a change in pay grade within the current pay plan.[3] Under this new definition, referred to here as *definition 2,* people who receive a promotion (i.e., move from GS-12 to GS-13) in conjunction with a switch into or out of the AW would be counted as substantive rather than administrative switches, even if they stay in the same occupational series and the same organization.

Definition 2 reclassifies approximately 10 percent of the total recategorizations from the administrative to the substantive category relative to definition 1. The percentage of switches that are classified as administrative is always slightly lower under definition 2.

The implementation and eventual revocation of the National Security Personnel System (NSPS) posed a more serious challenge for our original definition of substantive switches.

---

[3]   Since pay plan is a trigger, an individual switcher whose pay grade changes along with a change in pay plan is already being counted as a substantive switch.

The FY 2004 National Defense Authorization Act (NDAA) (Public Law 108-136) gave the Secretary of Defense the authority to work with the Office of Personnel Management (OPM) to establish a new, flexible human resources system covering the civilian defense workforce.[4] Using this authority, DoD established the NSPS. DoD began converting personnel into NSPS in 2006. Amid concerns about the implementation of NSPS, further expansion was put on hold in March 2009, pending the results of an independent review (DoD, 2009). That review, by the Defense Business Board (2009), identified some serious issues with the implementation of NSPS. DoD put a hold on any further conversions in NSPS.[5] The FY 2010 NDAA (Public Law 111-84) repealed NSPS and required DoD to move people out of NSPS pay plans by January 2012. At that point, about 226,000 DoD civilians were covered by an NSPS pay plan (Farrell, 2011). As a result, pay grade and pay plan changes continued to occur between FY 2010 and FY 2012. This resulted in a large number of pay plan and pay grade changes for AW personnel that were not related to any change in the nature of their jobs or the work they did. The NSPS conversion experience led us to consider whether pay plan conversions were in fact substantive and should be considered triggers for classifying a switch as substantive. Although NSPS was a DoD-wide initiative, other organizations have converted to alternative pay plans on a systematic basis since 1992. Such conversions involve pay plan changes for all eligible employees in a given organization. As a result, we decided that they did not in fact reflect a substantive change to the nature of work that a person was doing.

To address this issue, we constructed alternatives to definitions 1 and 2 described above. In these alternative definitions, pay plan is a trigger for classifying a switch as substantive *only* if the switch involved movement into or out of the Senior Executive Service (SES). Any other pay plan changes, such as movement from the General Schedule (GS) to an NSPS pay plan, are not a trigger for classifying a switch as substantive. A pay grade change is considered a trigger for a substantive switch *only* if there was also no change in pay plan. We imposed this qualification because different pay plans have different grade structures. So, a change in pay plan will almost always involve a change in pay grade, and it is impossible to tell whether that change is a promotion. Within a given pay plan, a change in pay grade does reflect a promotion (or a demotion). These alternative definitions are referred to as definitions 1a and 2a. Figure 2.2 describes the logic of these alternative definitions.

After developing these new definitions, we examined the number of switches that were classified as substantive and administrative under definitions 1, 2, 1a, and 2a for FYs 1993 through 2011. We also examined the number of switches in which NSPS pay plan changes or any pay plan changes other than those involving the SES were the only trigger for classifying a switch as substantive. This analysis revealed that, since 1992, there have been a small number of switches for which pay plan was the only trigger but that the number increased dramatically in the NSPS conversion years.

---

[4] The Civil Service Reform Act of 1978 (codified in Part 470 of USC Title 5) provides for federal agencies developing "demonstration" pay systems for the express purpose of testing the potential benefit of changes in personnel policies and procedures. These alternative systems (also referred to as *demonstration projects*) must be approved by OPM and are subject to review and evaluation. Although OPM approves the projects for a fixed duration, successful projects may be renewed and even be made permanent. Common elements of these projects include broadbanding (i.e., reducing the number of grade levels from 15 to 3–5), pay for performance, increased flexibility in hiring, and promotion decisions (Congressional Budget Office, 2008). NSPS included many features of older demonstration projects.

[5] A key concern was that the performance-based pay system used in NSPS was extremely complicated and lacking in transparency.

Figure 2.2
Revised Definitions of Substantive and Administrative Switching Into and Out of the Acquisition Workforce

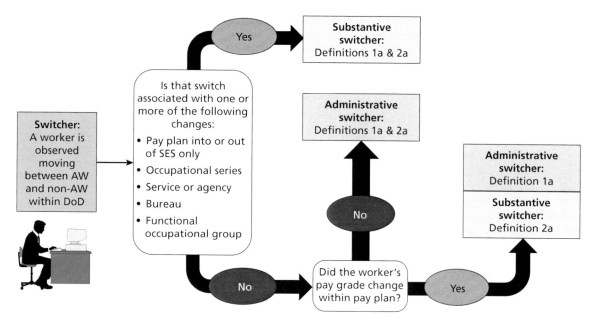

Definition 1a: Change in grade level within a pay plan is not a trigger for categorizing a switch as substantive.
Definition 2a: Change in grade level within a pay plan is a trigger for categorizing a switch as substantive.
RAND *RR110-2.2*

Given the vast numbers of people who have moved into and out of NSPS pay plans over this period and recognizing that these moves were administrative, we decided to use definition 2a—which includes promotions but excludes pay plan changes other than those that involve the SES from our definition of substantive switches—in the analysis presented in this report and in our analyses going forward.

The following are the main differences between definition 1 (the original definition) and definition 2a:

- Definition 2a counts a switcher who receives a promotion (change in grade level) within his current pay plan as a substantive switch, but definition 1 counts the individual as an administrative switch if nothing else changed in the same year.
- Definition 2a counts a switcher whose pay plan (and possibly pay grade) changes but whose personnel record had no other changes in the same year as an administrative switch, unless that person moved into or out of the SES.

Definition 2a has been incorporated into our analysis of FY 2011 data and will be used in our analyses henceforth when we distinguish between substantive and administrative switches. In this report, we describe the results of some sensitivity analyses we did looking at how the findings differ as a consequence of replacing definition 1 with definition 2a.

Definition of Substantive Switching Can Be Used in Subset Analysis of Career Field Populations

DoD policymakers are often interested in data on subsets of the AW—especially career fields, services, or agencies and career fields within services or agencies. When providing information on these subsets of the AW, we must modify our definition of switches into or out of the workforce. In this case, a *switcher* is anyone who moves into or out of the population of interest but remains employed by DoD. So, in the context of a career field–specific analysis, a person who switches from the SPRDE career field to the program management career field is identified as a switch out of the SPRDE career field and a switch into the program management career field. It is worth noting that, in the AT&L-wide analysis, this person would not have been identified as a switcher at all because he or she is part of the AW in both years. By definition, there will be more switching in and out in the career field projections than in the AW-wide projection model.

We use the same triggers to classify a switch as substantive or administrative in the career field analysis as we do in the overall analysis. If a person switches career fields within the AW but experiences no change in any of the trigger variables depicted in Figure 2.2, the change is classified as an administrative switch. Otherwise, the change is classified as a substantive switch.

Similarly, service-level analyses use a definition of switches that is similar to the one for the career field projections. A person moving between the Army AW and the Air Force AW, for example, will be counted as a switch out of the Army AW and a switch into the Air Force AW.[6] Because service or agency is a trigger variable for a substantive switch, all service or agency switches are automatically classified as substantive. Again, the total number of switches in service-level analyses will exceed the total number of switches into or out of the AW for the AT&L workforce as a whole because the analyses count switches between services or agencies, which are ignored in the AW-wide analyses.

Retirement Eligibility Is More Accurately Accounted For

The vast majority of civil servants DoD currently employs participate in one of two retirement plans: CSRS and FERS.[7] FERS was created in 1986; anyone hired into the federal civil service after January 1, 1987, is automatically covered under FERS. Employees hired prior to that date were covered by CSRS when they were hired but had the option to switch into FERS.

For the purposes of our analysis, we create a variable for each individual covered under either CSRS or FERS called *years of retirement eligibility* (YORE) or, more accurately, years relative to retirement eligibility. We do this by calculating the earliest age at which each individual could claim regular, full retirement benefits, given his or her current retirement plan, age, and YOS under the assumption that he or she will work continuously until that future retirement eligibility date and will remain covered under the current retirement plan. The age at which one can retire with full, regular benefits depends on the retirement plan, age, YOS,

---

[6]   If the person left the Army AW to work in any part of DoD outside the AW (the Army or another service), he or she would be counted as a switch out of the Army AW and would not be counted as a switch into any other AW group.

[7]   In FY 2011, 662 out of 136,066 civilian AW employees were covered by retirement plans other than CSRS or FERS.

and birth year, as described by OPM.[8] We then calculate the FY in which that individual will reach full, regular retirement eligibility. To calculate YORE for a particular FY, we subtract the FY of interest from the FY in which an individual reaches full retirement eligibility and add one. So for example, if an individual reaches full retirement eligibility in FY 2012, his or her YORE is –1 at the end of FY 2010, 0 at the end of FY 2011, and 1 at the end of FY 2012. Our YORE measure does not account for special retirement incentives that might result in optional retirement prior to reaching regular (full) retirement eligibility or disability retirement. For this reason, we do observe some people in the data set who retire before having reached regular retirement eligibility.

To summarize, individuals with YORE = 0 in a given year are those who become retirement-eligible for the first time in the next FY. The people in the data set with YORE = 0 at the end of FY 2011 were not yet retirement-eligible as of the end of FY 2011 but would become retirement-eligible before the end of FY 2012. Those with a negative YORE at the end of FY 2011 would not reach retirement eligibility during FY 2012; those with positive YORE have already attained retirement eligibility. When we report on turnover by YORE for a given FY, we reference YORE as measured at the end of the prior FY and report on the fraction of these people who leave before the end of the FY of interest.

In our prior report, we calculated YORE based on year of birth as reported in the personnel file. However, given the phase-in of higher MRA for FERS employees described earlier, the use of year of birth was causing inaccuracies for individuals born between 1948 and 1953 or between 1965 and 1969. Given the issues the MRA phase-in caused (described in footnote 12), we revised the way we calculated YORE in this report and now use the full date of birth.[9] When the date of birth is missing, we set the birthdate to *missing* and do not include these individuals in any analysis that involves the YORE variable.[10]

Differences in the Number of Observations Across Data Files Were Noted

By linking records across data files, we are able to perform analyses that are not possible in analyses of cross-sectional data. The process of linking data from multiple sources also uncovered some inconsistencies and other issues across files that require us to either drop records from the analysis or reclassify records. Over the past several years, we have been working to systematically document how and why the number of observations in our analyses differ from the number of records in the DAWIA person file that DoD has flagged as occupying an encumbered AW position. We then match the records contained in that file with the DoD civilian master file and the DoD military WEX file. We included in the civilian analysis all people who are in both the DMDC civilian personnel master file and in the DAWIA person

---

[8] Individuals who are covered under FERS and achieve 30 YOS must also reach a minimum retirement age (MRA) before they qualify for full retirement benefits. That minimum age depends on birth year. It was 55 for those born before 1948; 56 for those born between 1953 and 1964, and 57 for those born after 1969. Individuals born between 1948 and 1953 or between 1965 and 1969 were part of a phase-in process to the higher years. MRA depends on age in months. (See OPM, undated b.)

[9] In the September 2011 civilian data, we fixed 496 leap-year birthdates: DMDC delivered these cases with day of birth set to 0, instead of 29. In all other years, when day of birth is missing, we imputed a legitimate value.

[10] For a total of 2,482 individuals, we observed no birth date in any year between 1992 and 2009. Ninety-nine percent of these cases are prior to 2004. There are no missing birth dates after 2009.

file as of the end of the FY. We included in the military analysis all people who are in both the DMDC military WEX file and the DAWIA person file and not also in the civilian inventory file as of the end of the FY.

The DAWIA person file does contain an indicator of whether an individual is military or civilian. We have found slight discrepancies between the indicator in the DAWIA file and the data contained in the civilian and military files. We have been working to resolve such discrepancies and next document how we deal with suspicious cases.

First, some people match both the civilian inventory and the military WEX file. These individuals appear to be reservists, and we have counted them as members of the civilian, rather than the military, AW. Of the 5,095 such people in FY 2011, 5,062 were originally categorized as civilians in the DAWIA. Second, some people appear as military in the DAWIA file but match only to the end-of-year civilian inventory file (or vice versa). Our review of the cases indicates that the DAWIA file is not being updated immediately to reflect changes in status (i.e., a person separates from the military and is hired as a civilian).[11] As such, when individuals appear in the DAWIA data but their status code does not match the workforce of which they are a part, we recode their AW status to reflect the workforce of which they are a part, based on their presence in the civilian or WEX files. For example, if a person appears in the DAWIA file with a civilian flag, does not appear in the civilian inventory file, but does appear in the military WEX file, we consider that person to be part of the military AW. We found one person coded as military in the DAWIA file for FY 2011 who appeared in the civilian file but not in the military file; we found ten coded as civilian in that file who appeared in the military file but not in the civilian file.

Finally, there are individuals who appear in the DAWIA file but do not match to either the WEX or the civilian inventory file. We dropped these records from the analysis. Our review indicates that these are cases where the person has separated from DoD but is still appearing in the DAWIA file. For FY 2011, we found 414 such cases.

The three-stage process described above led to a core analytical file that we used to analyze gains and losses and to generate descriptive information about the AW. Some of the analyses we do, including notably the inventory projections, rely on information about an individual's YORE. For these analyses, we drop individuals whose retirement plan indicator is "other" because we are not able to calculate a YORE variable for these people. In FY 2011, 662 out of 136,066 civilian AW employees were covered by retirement plans other than CSRS or FERS.[12]

---

[11] By policy, DoD components report AW workforce data on a quarterly basis, while the civilian and military personnel files are updated on a just-in-time basis, when a transaction occurs. This distinction in reporting may contribute to the discrepancies we have observed.

[12] Of these 662 observations that are not part of CSRS or FERS, a majority are covered by the Social Security System, with no other retirement benefit. Other observations are simply missing data in this field, or are coded as "none" or "other" in the DMDC data.

CHAPTER THREE

DoD Civilian Acquisition Workforce Descriptive Overview FY 2011

This chapter provides updates to descriptive analyses presented in Gates et al., 2008. We describe the current state and highlight differences between the FY 2011 civilian AW and the FY 2006 civilian AW. The AW growth initiative reflected a major DoD policy shift, and managers and policymakers can use this updated information to assess the extent to which the growth goals are being achieved. In addition, updated workforce information provides managers with insights into the effects of the Great Recession on attrition. In this chapter, we also describe the defense science, technology, engineering, and mathematics (STEM) workforce. There is substantial overlap between the STEM workforce and the AW. The DoD STEM workforce has received attention from the National Academy of Engineering and the National Research Council. Because DoD engages in workforce planning for the STEM workforce separately from AW planning, this summary of the degree of overlap between the DoD STEM workforce and the AW may be of interest to policymakers as they interpret these separate workforce planning efforts.

Civilian Acquisition Workforce Growth Was Consistent with Growth Initiative

Figure 3.1 displays the civilian AW end-of-FY totals as tallied from service or agency submissions made in accordance with DoDI 5000.55 (i.e., the DAWIA counts). As mentioned in Chapter Two, the methods used to identify members of the AW for the DAWIA counts prior to 2005 differ from those used in the earlier period. As discussed at length in Gates (2009) and as reflected in Figure 3.6 later in this chapter, DoD recategorized a significant number of positions (particularly in the scientist and engineering occupations) into the AW in the late 1990s and early 2000s as part of a focused effort to align the Refined Packard definition with the DAWIA count referred to as assimilation (see DoD, 2010, p. 2-7). For this reason, policymakers are urged to use caution in interpreting broad workforce trends based on the DAWIA count prior to 2005 and to take account of the recategorizations that occurred.

The civilian AW, as measured by the DAWIA count, hit a low of 77,504 as of September 30, 1999, climbed steadily to 119,251 as of September 30, 2005, and declined again to 111,495 in FY 2008. As mentioned earlier, one key objective of the AW growth initiative is to increase the size of the organic AW by 20,000 between 2008 and 2015. Our analysis reveals that, as of the end of FY 2011, the civilian AW stood at 136,066—approximately 25,000 above the FY 2008 level.

Figure 3.1
Civilians in the DAWIA Workforce, September 30 Annual Snapshots

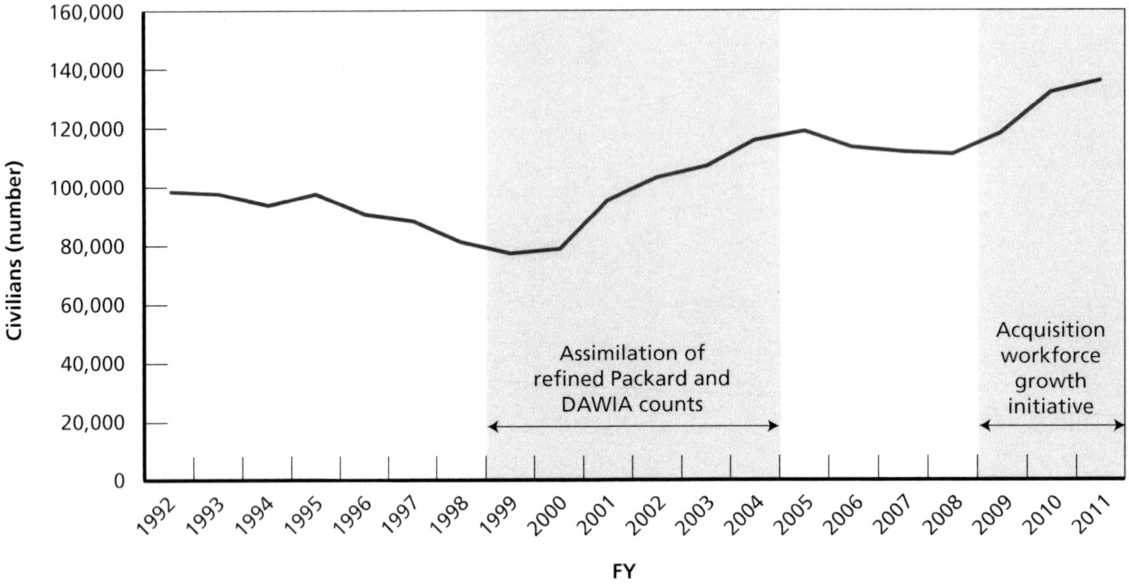

Figure 3.2 shows the total DoD civilian workforce over the same time frame and reveals somewhat different trends. The total civilian workforce declined steadily and dramatically from a high of 980,269 in FY 1992 to a low of 668,457 in FY 2001. Except for a slight dip between FYs 2006 and 2007, the total DoD civilian workforce has increased since FY 2001, to 788,289 in FY 2011.

In FY 2011, the civilian AW comprised 17 percent of the overall DoD civilian workforce. Prior to FY 2001, the AW had accounted for 10 to 12 percent of the DoD civilian workforce. Between FYs 2001 and 2003, the AW share increased 16 percent and has fluctuated between 16 and 18 percent since that time.

Analysis by Service Indicates That the Navy Employs the Most AW Civilians

Figure 3.3 reports the number of AW employees by service or agency in FY 2011. Figure 3.3, shows that, FY 2011, the Army employed approximately one-third of AW civilians; the Navy employed one-third; and the Marine Corps, the Air Force, or the Office of the Secretary of Defense and the defense agencies employed the remaining 36 percent. Figure 3.4 reflects the distribution of the AW across components as of FY 2006. A comparison of the two charts reveals where much of the workforce growth has occurred. The percentage of the total civilian AW the Army employs has declined by 9 percentage points since FY 2006, when it stood at 39 percent.

Experience Gap Between AW and DoD Civilians Seems to Be Closing

Figure 3.5 presents the distribution of AW and DoD civilians by YOS in the federal government as civilian employees. As was true in FY 2006, AW civilians tend to have more experience than is typical for DoD overall. However, the difference between the AW and other DoD civilians is not as dramatic as it once was. The growth in both workforces has also led to a

Figure 3.2
Civilians in the DoD Workforce, September 30 Annual Snapshots

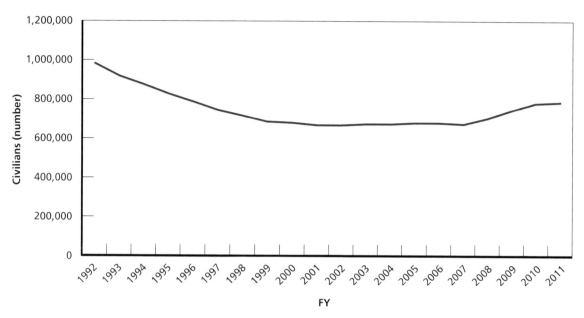

RAND *RR1100-3.2*

Figure 3.3
AW Civilian Inventory, by Service or Agency, 2011

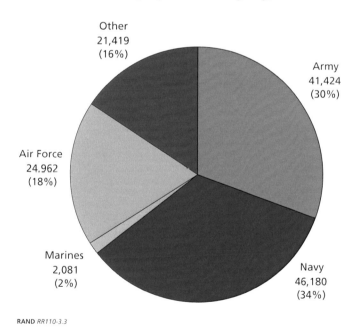

RAND *RR110-3.3*

change in the YOS distribution. In FY 2011, close to one-half of both workforces had fewer than ten years of federal service. It is worth emphasizing that individuals with fewer than ten years of federal service as civilian workers are not necessarily "inexperienced." New civilian hires may enter the workforce with experience (sometimes substantial) in the private sector or in the military.

Figure 3.4
AW Civilian Inventory, by Service or Agency, 2006

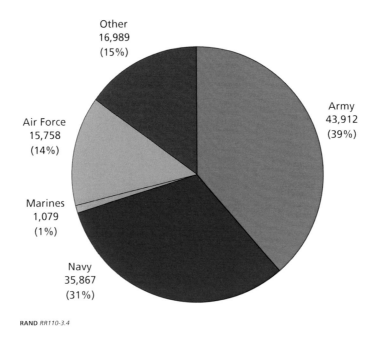

RAND *RR110-3.4*

Figure 3.5
Civilian Acquisition and DoD-Wide Workforce Years of Service Levels, FY 2011

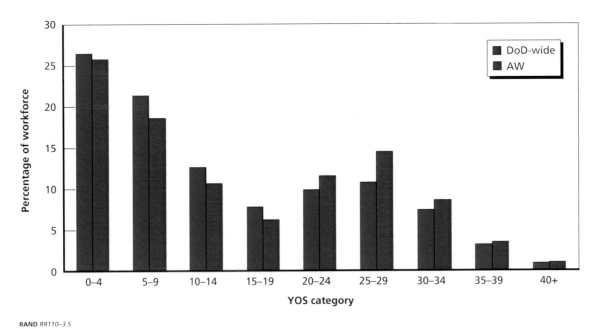

RAND *RR110–3.5*

In FY 2006, there was a dearth of civilian workers with five to 14 years of experience, both in the AW and DoD-wide, likely as a result of the post–Cold War DoD drawdown that resulted in limited civilian hiring in the 1990s (Gates et al., 2008, p. 13). Today, a similar trough exists among workers with 10 to 24 years of experience.

Systems Planning; Research, Development, and Engineering; and Contracting Are the Largest Career Fields

It is also useful to consider the activities the civilian AW performs, as reflected by its acquisition career fields. Figure 3.6 illustrates that systems planning; research, development, and engineering; and contracting are the largest career fields, employing nearly one-half the civilian AW. However, the share of the workforce in these two career fields has decreased since FY 2006, when they employed 30 percent and 22 percent of the workforce, respectively (Gates et al., 2008, p. 14).

AW May Face Looming Retirement Wave

Figure 3.7 shows the workforce distribution by YORE as of September 30, 2011. In this display, a person with YORE = 1 became retirement-eligible during FY 2011. A person at YORE = 0 did not become retirement-eligible in FY 2011 but would be eligible in FY 2012.

In our prior report, we noted that, starting in FY 2007, about 4 percent of both the DoD and AW civilian workforces would be achieving retirement eligibility each year and that this increase in retirement eligibility would last for about a decade (Gates et al., 2008, pp. 14–15). Figure 3.7 reveals that this trend is expected to continue in the civilian AW but that the percentage of workers at or nearing retirement eligibility will be slightly lower for the DoD-wide civilian workforce.

Career Recategorizations Tend to Exceed the Number of New Hires

Figure 3.1 showed fairly marked growth in the size of the civilian AW in recent years. Figure 3.8 plots the number of new hires entering the AW, civilians already employed by DoD who were recategorized into the AW, recategorizations out of the AW, and attrition out of DoD among

Figure 3.6
Civilian AW by Career Field, 2011

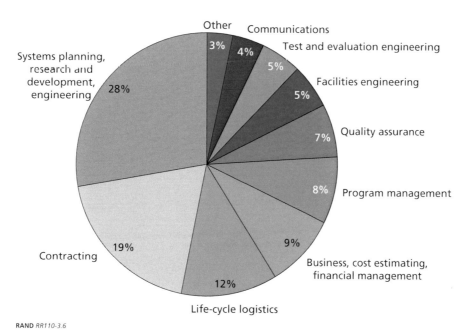

Figure 3.7
Percentage of Civilian Workers at or Nearing Retirement Eligibility, FY 2011

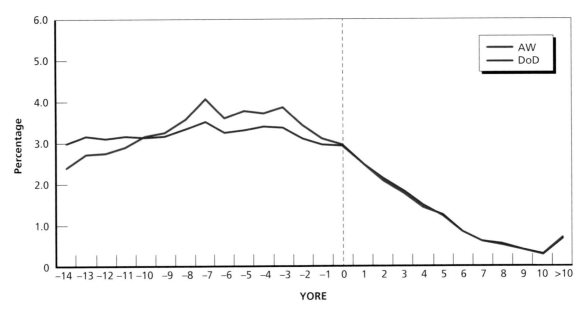

Figure 3.8
Entrances into and Exits from the Civilian Acquisition Workforce

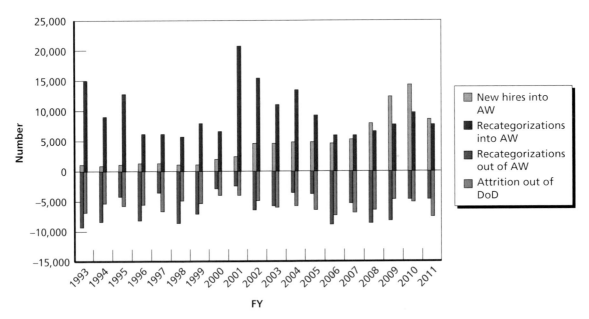

members of the civilian AW by FY. As previously described, recategorized AW civilians are those who transitioned into or out of the AW from a non-AW civilian position. This does not include those who transfer from the military or those who switch service or position within the AW.

Between FYs 1993 and 2007, the number of DoD employees who were recategorized into the AW exceeded the number of new hires into the AW from outside DoD, often by quite a lot. The highest number of recategorizations was during the assimilation period of the early 2000s, when DoD was actively working to ensure that positions were being counted accurately. The number of new hires began increasing in 2002; by 2008, the number of new hires exceeded the number of gains due to recategorizations.

Recategorizations out of the AW (while remaining employed by DoD) and attrition out of DoD have typically had magnitudes comparable to those for exits from DoD.

Figure 3.9 disaggregates the annual recategorization spikes by component (service or agency). This chart reveals that, since 2004, service-specific spikes in the number of recategorizations have declined. This suggests that the number of administrative recategorizations may have declined in recent years.

We also see that the largest spikes in recategorization are typically driven by a high level of recategorizations in one of the services. The large 2001 spike into the AW was predominantly from the Army (15,287 of 20,513), while the 2002 spike into the AW was predominantly from the Department of the Navy, which includes the Navy and the Marine Corps (8,117 of 15,247). FYs 2008 and 2009 saw a relatively high number of recategorizations out of the AW, primarily due to an increase in such outbound recategorizations by the Navy and the Army.

In Chapter Two, we described refinements to our definition of whether a switch into or out of the AW is categorized as administrative. Figures 3.10 and 3.11 illustrate the implications of that change in definition for the percentage of switches that are categorized as administrative. As illustrated in the figures, the new definition, 2a, results in a consistently lower percentage of switches being categorized as administrative through 2005. Starting in 2006, the definitions follow different patterns, reflecting the implications of the implementation of NSPS for our definitions. Switches in have the following pattern: Under definition 1, there is a slight

Figure 3.9
Civilian Recategorizations, by Component

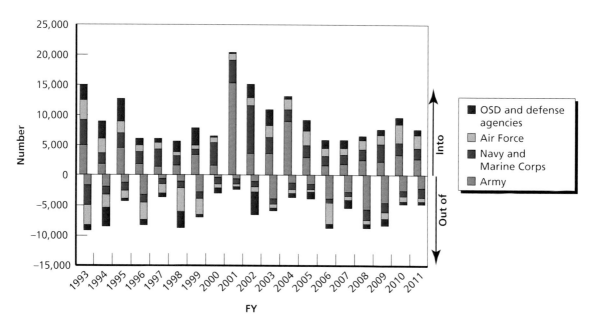

Figure 3.10
Percentage of Civilian AW Recategorizations In Classified as Administrative, by Definition

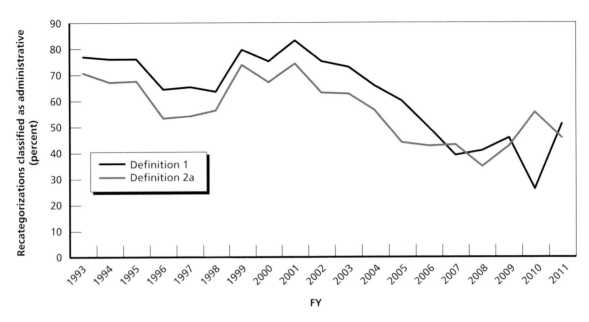

Figure 3.11
Percentage of Civilian AW Recategorizations Out Classified as Administrative, by Definition

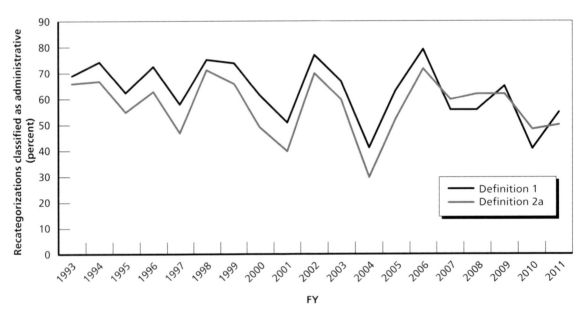

increase in the share that are administrative between 2006 and 2009, then a sharp decrease in the share that are administrative in FY 2010, and then a sharp increase in FY 2011. Under definition 2a, there was a steady decrease in the share classified as administrative through 2008, followed by an increase in FY 2009 and 2010, and then a decline in 2011. For switches out, the patterns are more comparable, although there is a striking difference between the pre- and post-2006 trends. Through FY 2006, the percentage of switches out classified as administrative is consistently lower under the new definition than under the original definition. After FY 2006, this is no longer the case.

Overall, and under both definitions, the share of switches that is administrative has declined overall (if not consistently). For FY 2011, about one-half of the switches are categorized as administrative.

As noted in our prior report, it is possible that there are substantive aspects of workers' jobs that change on entering or exiting the AW, but these aspects are not observed in the civilian personnel data. We have no way to evaluate this alternative possibility.

Acquisition Workforce Attrition Remains Low

Figures 3.12 and 3.13 provide information on the rate of exit or attrition from DoD employment and describe the share of total attrition due to retirement, voluntary separation, involuntary separation, and other reasons.[1] AW attrition out of DoD has been consistently lower than DoD civilian norms, largely due to lower voluntary and involuntary separations. Retirement rates (as a share of the total civilian workforce) have been comparable for AW civilians and all DoD civilians over time.

For both the AW and the overall civilian workforce, the rate of exit declined slightly in FY 2008, more significantly in FY 2009, remained low in FY 2010, and increased in FY 2011.

Figure 3.12
AW Civilian Workforce Attrition Rate, by Fiscal Year and Category

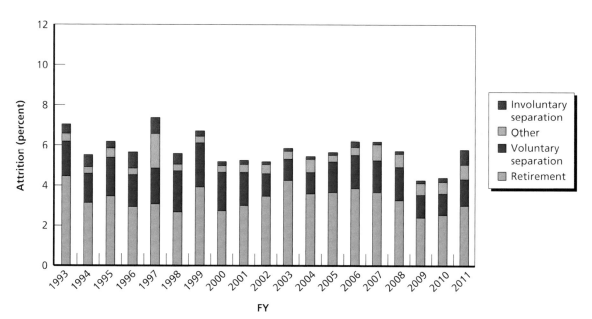

RAND RR110-3.12

_____

[1] "Other" includes observations for which a separation code is not recorded in the data in spite of the fact that the individual has left the data set.

Figure 3.13
DoD Civilian Workforce Attrition Rate, by Fiscal Year and Category

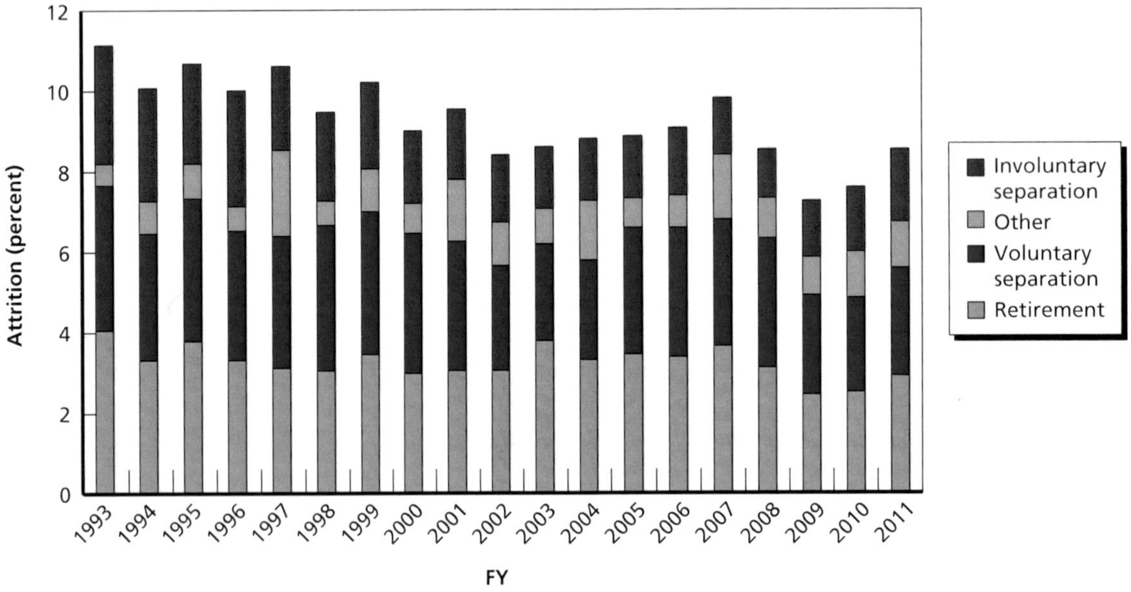

RAND RR110-3.13

FYs 2009 and 2010 saw unusually low rates of voluntary separation and retirement, likely due to high unemployment rates and concerns about stock market and pension valuations. We reported in Gates et al., 2008, that the AW seems to be characterized by lower attrition, even controlling for the different seniority and educational composition of the AW. These trends continued through the current period. Acquisition workers, simply put, appear to be attached to their jobs relative to other DoD civilian employees.

Various Factors Are Related to Attrition Rates

Within the AW, we observe different exit rates for different career fields. Figure 3.14 presents the attrition rates for the contracting career field, and Figure 3.15 presents similar information for SPRDE.

A comparison of Figures 3.14 and 3.15 shows that, since 2004, attrition rates have been about 2 percentage points higher for the contracting career field than for SPRDE. There were also a large number of separations for "other" reasons among members of the SPRDE career field in 1997.

In looking into this issue, we discovered that the vast majority of these separations were associated with Base Realignment and Closure IV. For example, functions performed at the Naval Air Warfare Center in Indianapolis, Indiana, were relocated to Patuxent River. Seven hundred and twenty-five employees who were based at NAWC in Indianapolis in 1996 separated from DoD (do not appear in the file in 1997), but no separation code was recorded in their files.

Not surprisingly, however, a surge in attrition occurs when civilian employees become fully retirement-eligible, both DoD-wide and in the AW. Figure 3.16 shows the rate of attrition (as a percentage of the prior-year baseline) by YORE. Workers with YORE = 0 are those who became retirement-eligible for the first time in FY 2011. The far left side of the graph reflects

Figure 3.14
AW Contracting Workforce Attrition Rate, by Fiscal Year and Category

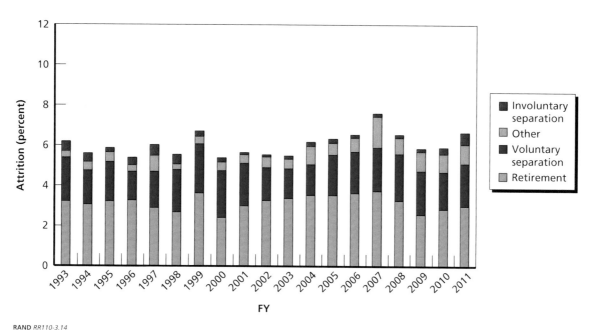

RAND RR110-3.14

Figure 3.15
AW SPRDE Workforce Attrition Rate, by Fiscal Year and Category

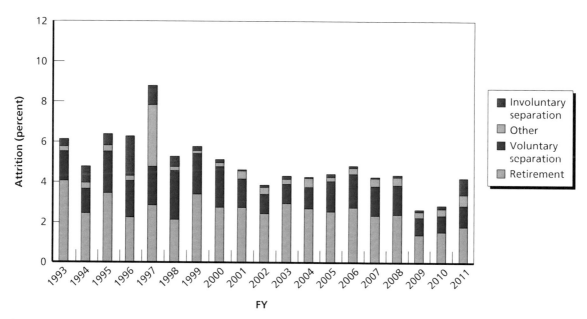

RAND RR110-3.15

those with a decade or more until retirement eligibility, while the far right reflects those who have been retirement-eligible for a decade or more but still remain employed by DoD. We have placed the vertical axis at the edge of Year 0, the first year of full retirement eligibility.

Along with the jump in attrition propensity upon becoming fully retirement-eligible, the AW (again) has lower attrition in the years preceding eligibility than the DoD workforce as

Figure 3.16
Civilian Attrition Rates by Years Relative to Retirement Eligibility, FY 2011

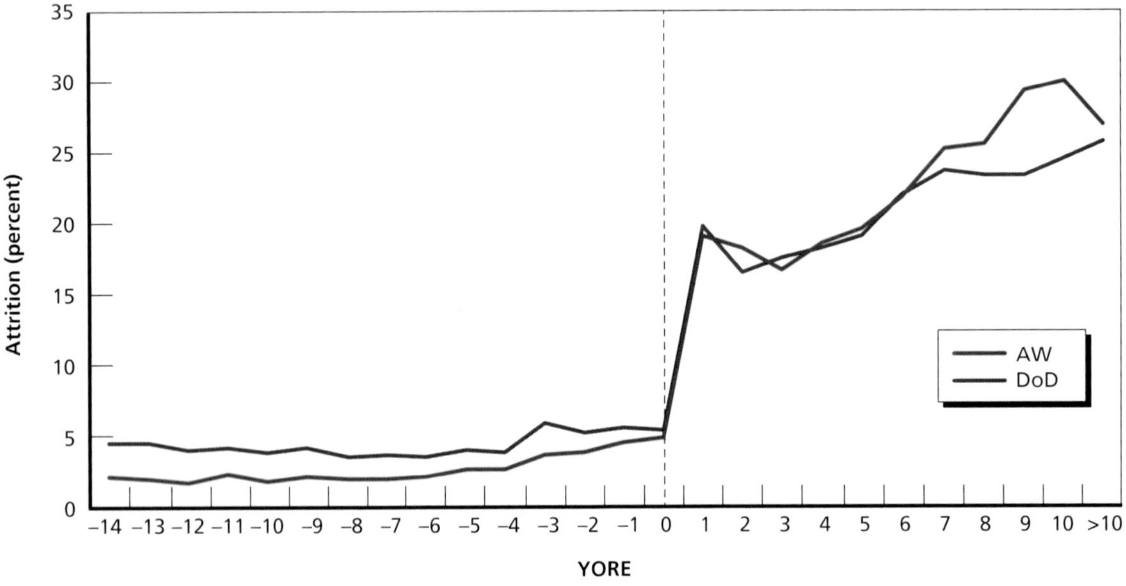

RAND *RR110-3.16*

a whole. The postretirement eligibility attrition behavior looks similar for AW and non-AW employees in FY 2011.

Type of Retirement Plan Affects Exit Rates

Given the differences between the two major retirement plans, the older, more-traditional CSRS and the newer FERS, it is important to consider whether the retirement behavior described in this section differs for individuals depending on the retirement plan. The plans differ notably in terms of benefits. Those covered by CSRS are not eligible for Social Security benefits based on their federal employment. FERS has a defined benefit and a defined contribution component. In addition, individuals covered under FERS also receive Social Security credits. Under CSRS, employees who leave federal employment before they reach retirement age receive no retirement benefits. Thus, the plan creates very strong incentives for employees to remain in the civil service. These incentives do not exist with FERS to the same extent, since all employees receive a government contribution to their Thrift Savings Account (similar to a 401K account), and employees with as few as five YOS are eligible for a basic benefit annuity payment when they reach retirement age (OPM, 1997).

Figure 3.17 shows the attrition rate by YORE for CSRS and FERS employees in the AW during FY 2011.

In FY 2006, AW civilians in CSRS generally had lower attrition rates before retirement eligibility but then a bigger attrition jump upon achieving eligibility relative to FERS AW civilians (Gates et al., 2008, p. 21). In FY 2011, rates of attrition are lower among FERS employees both prior to and after retirement eligibility. This may reflect a response to declining retirement fund values among FERS employees or may also be due to broader demographic differences between the nearly retirement-eligible FERS and CSRS populations.

**Figure 3.17
Civilian AW Attrition Rate, by Years Relative to Retirement Eligibility
and Retirement Plan, FY 2011**

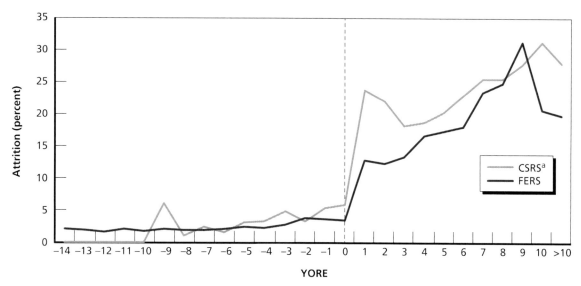

a Due to the phasing out of CSRS, there are fewer than 100 individuals in each YORE category beyond –8.
This leads to greater variation in attrition rates for these groups.
RAND RR110-3.17

Science, Technology, Engineering, and Mathematics Personnel Compose Almost One-Half of Acquisition Workforce

Just as DoD devotes substantial attention to the management of the segment of the civilian workforce responsible for acquisition-related activities, it also pays special attention to the STEM workforce. For the purposes of this analysis, we define an employee as being part of the STEM workforce if he or she works in an occupational series that begins with 4, 8, 13, or 15. The 4xx series includes biological sciences; the 8xx includes engineering occupations; 13xx includes physical sciences; and 15xx includes mathematics, statistics, and computer sciences. For the purposes of this analysis, the definition of the STEM workforce does not include medical professionals (who are part of the 6xx series) or social scientists.

There is significant overlap between the AW and STEM DoD civilian workforces. As Figures 3.18 and 3.19 show, roughly one-half of DoD AW civilians are in STEM occupations, and roughly one-half of the DoD STEM workforce is also part of the AW.

At the end of FY 2011, 118,070 DoD civilian employees were in STEM occupations, of whom 57,010 were part of the AW; 136,066 were in the AW (STEM and non-STEM). As Figure 3.20 shows, approximately 25 percent of the DoD civilian workforce is in either STEM or AW; 17 percent is AW; 15 percent is STEM; 7 percent is both STEM and AW; and another 8 percent is STEM but not AW.

Figure 3.21 presents the attrition rates for the AW STEM workforce, and Figure 3.22 presents similar information for the overall DoD STEM workforce.

As is true of the overall workforce, the attrition rate for AW employees within the STEM workforce is lower than for DoD employees overall.

Figure 3.18
DoD AW Civilian Workforce, by STEM and Non-STEM, FY 2011

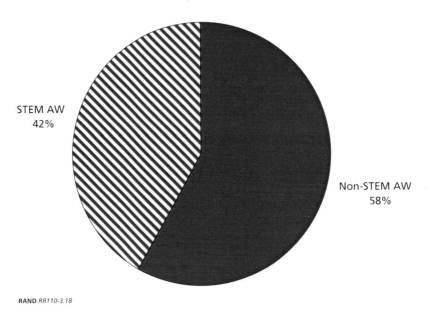

STEM AW
42%

Non-STEM AW
58%

RAND *RR110-3.18*

Figure 3.19
DoD Civilian STEM Workforce, by AW and Non-AW, FY 2011

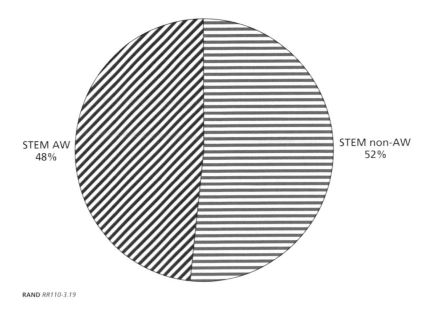

STEM AW
48%

STEM non-AW
52%

RAND *RR110-3.19*

STEM Workforce Overall Has High Retention

The average new hire and separation rates between 2007 and 2011 for the AW STEM population were slightly lower (by about 20 percent) than those for the overall AW and DoD-wide STEM populations. In analyses not reported here (but available from authors upon request), this was consistently true for both FERS and CSRS populations across the YORE distribution. Thus, the AW STEM workforce has slightly higher retention than either the overall AW population or the DoD-wide STEM population. As noted in the discussion of Figure 3.15, the spike in separations in 1997 appears to be due to Base Realignment and Closure issues.

Figure 3.20
DoD Civilian Workforce, by STEM and AW Status, FY 2011

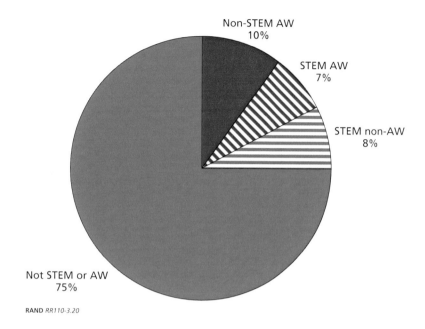

RAND *RR110-3.20*

Figure 3.21
AW STEM Workforce Attrition Rate, by Fiscal Year and Category

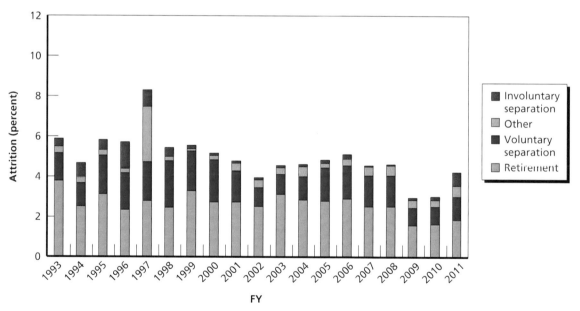

RAND *RR110-3.21*

Figure 3.22
DoD STEM Workforce Attrition Rate, by Fiscal Year and Category

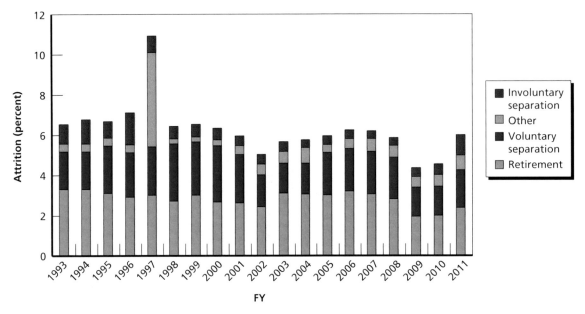

CHAPTER FOUR

Projections for the Civilian Acquisition Workforce

This chapter presents results from our updated DoD AW projections and for important workforce subcomponents. We used a modified version of the model described in Gates et al., 2008. The new version of the projection model differs from the prior version in two important respects. First, the model is now based on YORE rather than YOS. As described in Gates et al., 2008, YORE is more strongly correlated with separation rate. Regular retirement eligibility is determined by three factors: YOS, age, and retirement plan. These factors combined are more strongly correlated with retention than YOS alone. Second, we added an alternative version of the projection model to the worksheet that allows the user to input a target workforce size each year for the next ten years. Version 2 projects the number of new hires necessary to achieve, or at least approach, that goal. "Version 1" refers to the original projection tool, which was based on historical averages.

The supply projection models should be viewed as a tool rather than a prediction. The models make a number of default assumptions; for example, continuation and gain rates are based on average, historic civilian gains and losses over the past five years. Using these base rates, the models project what various aspects of the workforce will look like in the future if past trends carry forward into the future.

There are many reasons that future gain and loss rates would not be the same as historic averages. Importantly, the supply projection model does not account for changes in workforce demand. What it does do is provide managers insight into the retention patterns for a particular workforce and the implications of the patterns. Indeed, one key role for personnel managers is comparing workforce demand with the supply projection and determining whether some intervention, such as hiring or separation incentives, might be needed to balance supply and demand.

This chapter describes how the projections vary depending on assumptions about future hiring rates. We describe why the high hiring rates of the last few years are unlikely to continue. We then present workforce projections for a number of AW subpopulations using a new hire rate that is closer to the long-run historical average. Finally, we illustrate how managers can use the model to explore the implications of different future scenarios by walking through some plausible examples.

Appendix A provides the technical details for the new projection methodology.

The Projection Model Can Be Used to Explore Expected Workforce Growth Under Different Circumstances

We use the projection model to generate AW projections for three different scenarios. Figure 4.1 summarizes the projection results. The base model uses average rates of separation over the prior five FYs to generate the ten-year inventory projection.[1] The baseline workforce size used for the projection models is 135,320 for FY 2011. Between FY 2006 and FY 2011, the average hiring rate was 8 percent. The base model projection using that average hiring rate of 8 percent suggests that, if historical gain and separation rates by YORE hold over the next decade, the civilian AW will grow substantially over the next ten years, reaching over 213,132 by 2021.[2] This projected growth is driven by the dramatic growth in the AW between 2006 and 2011, combined with unusually high retention rates in FYs 2007 through 2011 due to the economic recession. The unusual gain and loss rates over the recent period may not be expected to continue into the future. Users may therefore wish to modify some of the model assumptions. Appendix A includes the procedures for doing so.

Alternative Projection Scenarios Result in More-Stable Population Sizes

Following these procedures, we generated projections for two alternative scenarios (see Figure 4.1). Assuming a new hire rate of 3 percent per year, the projection model indicates that the AW will *decline* to 126,355 by FY 2021. Assuming a hiring rate of 4 percent per year leads to a prediction of slight workforce growth, to 140,909 by FY 2021.

Base Model Projections by Career Field and Service or Agency Suggest Growth in All Areas

In addition to the DoD-wide projection models, we generated separate workbooks, which are also available from the authors on request, which provide inventory projection models for the DoD civilian AW by acquisition career field and by service or DoD agency. Because of the dramatic growth in the AW, the base model projections using the historical averages project significant growth for all subpopulations. Rather than present the default projections, this section reports the results of the projection models assuming a 4-percent new hire rate. As discussed earlier, when applied to the overall AW, this assumption yields a projection of modest and consistent workforce growth through 2021.

In the process of generating the projection models, we also produced summary data sheets that describe the total gains and losses, by type, for the past several years. We will present this

---

[1] As noted above, users may wish to use different separation rates in the model, for example, the three-year average separation rate or simply the separation rate from the previous year. The model can be easily adjusted to use these average separation rates. Different assumptions have their own pros and cons, and managers with an intimate knowledge of the historical trends for their particular workforces will be in the best position to judge which historical rates are the most appropriate inputs for the model. However, because the separation rates are calculated for each YORE group, the rates for a single year may be highly variable—especially for small subsegments of the workforce (e.g., specific career fields or occupational groups within specific commands).

[2] It is worth noting that the different switch definitions do not have major implications for the ten-year projections. Models using the alternative definitions described in Chapter Two generated the following predictions: 214,494 for definition 1 (original definition); 219,348 for definition 2; and 213,237 for definition 1a.

Figure 4.1
Projection of the Size of the DoD Civilian Acquisition Workforce, FY 2011–2021, Assuming Different Hiring Rates

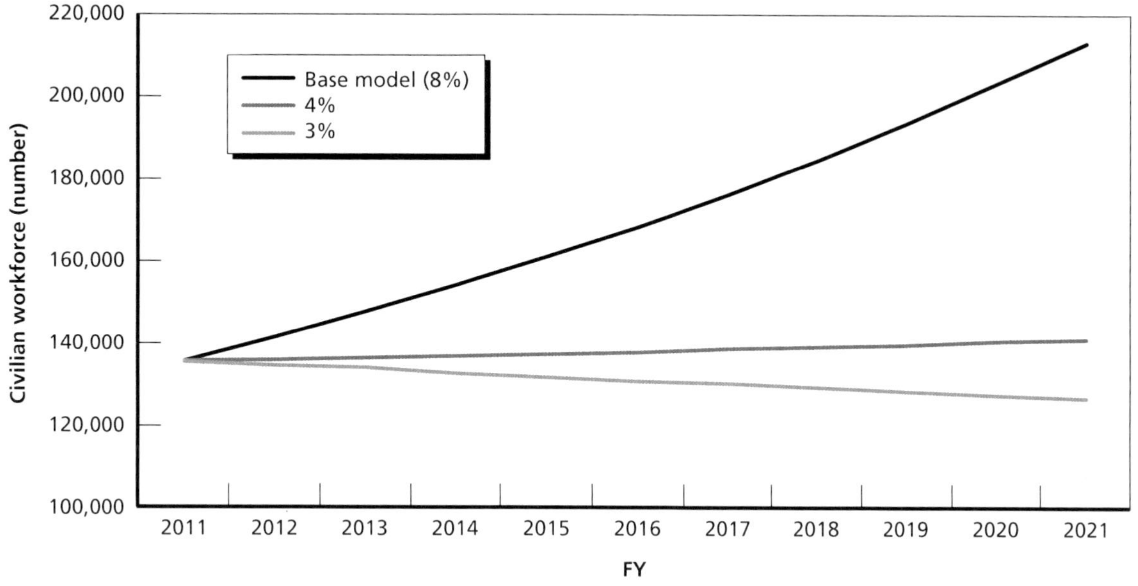

RAND RR110-4.1

information for selected subsets of the population to provide a sense of how trends differ across workforce subsets.

Career Field Projections Using a Plausible Alternate Assumption Show Workforce Gains in Some Fields, Losses in Others

Figures 4.2 through 4.4 present the results of the projection model (assuming a 4-percent new hire rate) by AW career field. For presentational purposes, we divide the career fields into three separate figures based on the size of the workforce in FY 2011.

The model projects that a 4-percent new hire rate would generate gains in some career fields and losses in others. The career fields that experience losses are those that have a higher than average rate of exit, a low rate of switching into the career field, and/or a high rate of switching out. For example, contracting has a consistently higher rate of exit than other career fields, and the model suggests that a higher hiring rate may be needed to maintain that workforce. Audit has a low rate of switching in and a somewhat high exit rate. Information technology has a relatively high rate of switching out. For these career fields, a slightly higher rate of new hires may be needed to maintain the workforce. The career fields that are projected to experience gains are those that have had a high rate of switching into the career field in recent years. In some cases (such as program management and logistics), this is a relatively consistent trend over time. If managers expect the historical rate of switching in to continue, they may conclude that a somewhat lower rate of new hires is needed to maintain the size of the workforce. In other cases, such as with science and technology, a newly created career field experienced a burst of growth through the rapid transfer of personnel from another career field. This rate of switching in may not be expected to continue into the future, and managers may wish to adjust the switch-in rates for the model accordingly.

Figure 4.2
Projection of the Size of the DoD Civilian Acquisition Workforce, FY 2011–2021, by Career Field, Assuming 4-Percent New Hire Rate, Part 1

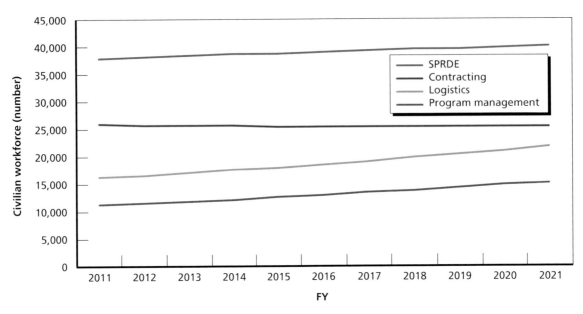

Figure 4.3
Projection of the Size of the DoD Civilian Acquisition Workforce, FY 2011–2021, by Career Field, Assuming 4-Percent New Hire Rate, Part 2

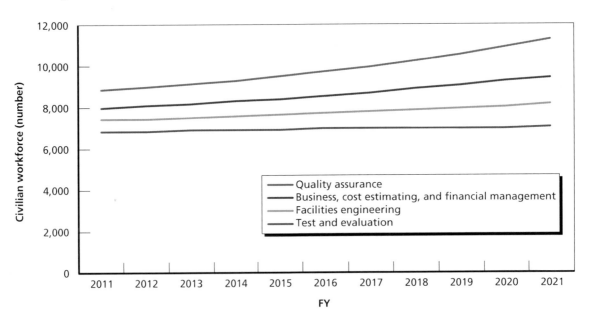

Figure 4.4
Projection of the Size of the DoD Civilian Acquisition Workforce, FY 2011–2021, by Career Field, Assuming 4-Percent New Hire Rate, Part 3

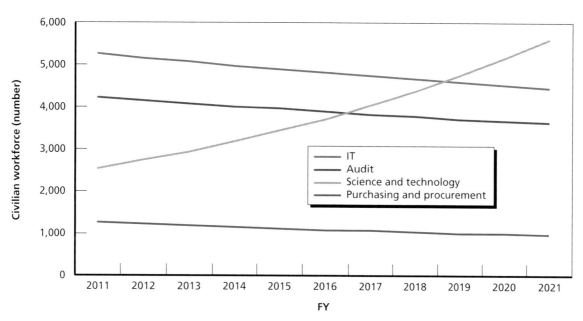

Five-Year Historical Average Gain and Loss Rates Are Highly Influenced by High Gain and Low Loss Rates for 2009 and 2010

A review of recent gain and loss patterns for the overall AW and for key AW career fields reveals that, in FYs 2009 and 2010, the number of new hires was high and that the number of exits from DoD was low (see Appendix B). Similarly, new hire *rates* were typically higher and exit *rates* typically lower for these years. Historical averages suggest substantial workforce growth for all the career fields. The data reveal some differences in the dynamics across the career fields described above. For example, in the program management career field, the proportion of total gains due to new hires increased from 21 percent in 2007 to 42 percent in 2011 (and was over 50 percent in 2010), indicating an increased emphasis on gains through external hiring rather than internal transfers (see Table B.1). The proportion of losses from the program management career field that are exits from DoD is low relative to other AW career fields. Approximately one-third of losses are due to exits from DoD, and two-thirds are due to switches out—either switches to other career fields or switches out of the AW.

The number of new hires into the SPRDE career field was twice as high in 2009 and 2010 as in the years before and after. In addition, the number of exits was very low for 2009 and 2010. Total switches in and out were high in 2010 relative to other years. Exit rates are below the AW-wide average for this career field. Exit rates are also low for the test and evaluation career field. The contracting career field consistently has higher exit rates than the overall AW.

The audit career field had a very high number of switches in in 2008, perhaps due to some systematic reclassification of employees into this career field. Managers should carefully consider the baseline assumptions for this projection. With the exception of 2008, switching in and out of this career field has been rare. A very high share of gains and losses is due to new hires and exits relative to other career fields. Also, exit rates were fairly high (6 percent) in 2009 and 2010.

Component Projections Based on Plausible Hiring Rate Assumptions Suggest Losses in the Defense Contract Audit Agency, Growth in the Defense Logistics Agency

Figures 4.5 and 4.6 present the results of the projection model (assuming a 4-percent new hire rate) by DoD component. For presentational purposes, we divided the service and component projections into two figures based on the size of the workforce in FY 2011.

As was true for the career field projections, the model projects that a 4-percent new hire rate would generate gains in some components and losses in others. The component that experiences projected losses (the Defense Contract Audit Agency) has experienced extremely little switching into its workforce in the last five years. Because the model anticipates a low number of "internal hires," a 4-percent new hire rate from outside DoD would not be sufficient to maintain the size of the workforce. The components that are projected to experience gains are those with high switch-in rates in recent years. In some cases (such as the Defense Logistics Agency [DLA]), this is a relatively consistent trend over time. If managers expect the historical switch-in rate to continue, they may conclude that rate of new hires to maintain the size of the workforce can be somewhat lower. In other cases, such as with the Missile Defense Agency (MDA), an agency has grown substantially in the past five years, through both higher than average hiring rates and the rapid transfer of personnel. This rate of switching in may not be expected to continue into the future, and managers may wish to adjust the switch-in rates for the model accordingly.

Figure 4.5
Projection of the Size of the DoD Civilian Acquisition Workforce, FY 2011–2021, by Component, Assuming 4-Percent New Hire Rate, Part 1

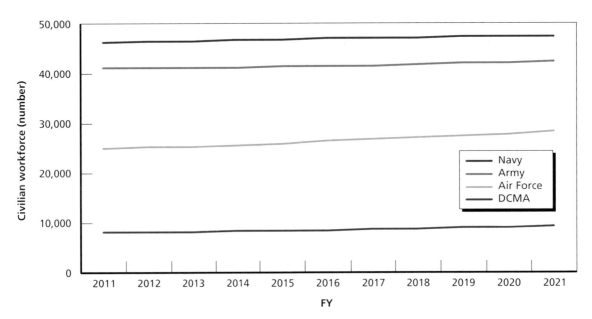

Figure 4.6
Projection of the Size of the DoD Civilian Acquisition Workforce, FY 2011–2021, by Component Assuming 4-Percent New Hire Rate, Part 2

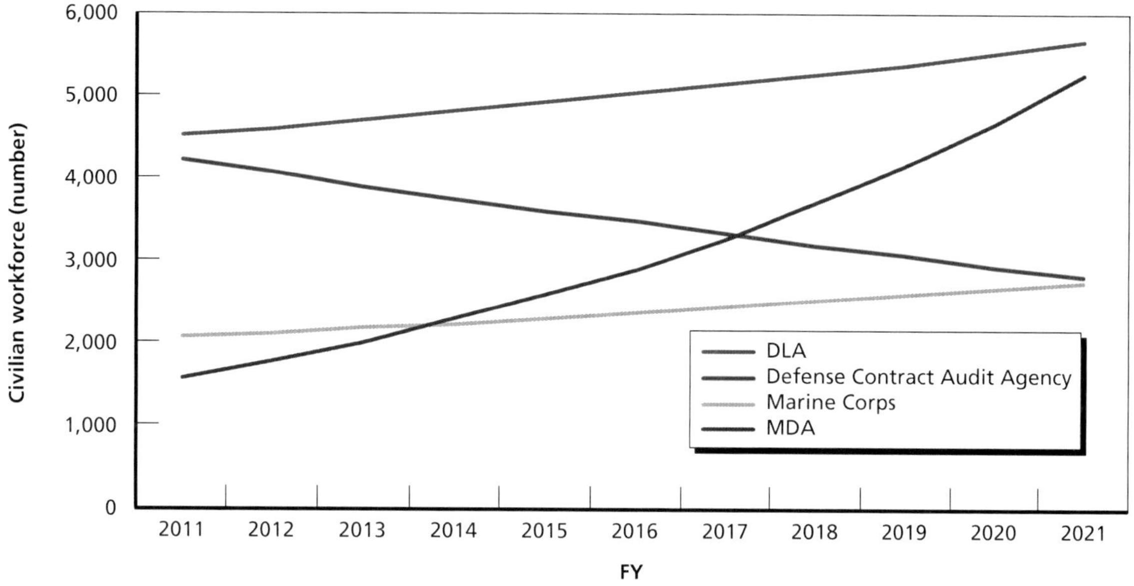

FY 2011 Acquisition Workforce Gain and Loss Patterns Vary by Service

The Army and the Defense Contract Management Agency (DCMA) are the only services or agencies that saw declines (–1.35 percent for Army and –0.6 percent for DCMA) in the size of the civilian AW for FY 2011 (see Appendix B). Both components had an exit rate of 8 percent in FY 2011, which exceeded the average rate for the AW. Examining the loss rates for the Army in greater detail, we found that loss rates for CSRS employees were much higher than in prior years (around 30 percent for those who are retirement eligible and well above 10 percent for those with YORE –1 and –2). This suggests that there may have been an explicit effort to encourage the separation of those who were eligible for retirement or close to eligibility and that CSRS employees were more sensitive to these efforts.

The Air Force and MDA had a higher than average rate of increase in the size of the civilian AW for 2011 (11 percent for AF and 12 percent for MDA). Both components had a higher than average new hire rate (9 percent for Air Force and 17 percent for MDA). DLA and the Air Force had a high rate of switching in (roughly 10 percent of the baseline).

Manipulating the Projection Model to Address a Range of Scenarios

The value of the workforce projection model lies in its flexibility, which allows managers to explore alternative scenarios by entering alternative continuation or gain rates. We have shown how the base model provides important information about the effects of one type of policy change—setting a fixed hiring rate at varying levels—on overall end strength. We have also demonstrated how the tool can be used for workforce analysis with specific populations, such as career fields. Yet there is a wide range of other options for adjusting the model to meet workforce management needs. This section describes how managers can manipulate the projection model to explore the potential workforce implications of some plausible scenarios.

It is important to emphasize that these models cannot predict the direction and magnitude of changes in gain or loss rates or distributions because these will be influenced by policy decisions and economic conditions that the model cannot anticipate. Managers must determine how to alter the model's rates and distributions, using their own best judgment to adjust the model parameters as needed to reflect expected future conditions. In this section, we describe how managers can adjust the model parameters to explore different scenarios.

Scenario 1

DoD wants to maintain the overall size of the AW at its current level and needs to know how to adjust hiring to meet these targets.

Under this scenario, the workforce manager has future end strength targets for the civilian workforce and wants to know how to adjust hiring to achieve these targets. Version 2 of the model is the appropriate tool for the analysis. To determine how many new hires will be needed to maintain end strength at current levels, the manager should enter the current FY end strength (in this case 135,320) as the target population size (see the highlighted cells in row 49 of Version 2 in the model—Figure 4.7). The output, highlighted in orange, indicates that DoD will require 4,994 new civilians to maintain end strength in FY 2012, a new hire rate of 3.7 percent. The number of accessions required to maintain end strength decreases slightly over time, to 4,751 new hires in 2021 (3.5 percent).

Scenario 2

DoD has end strength targets that vary over time and needs to know how to adjust accessions to meet these targets.

As with Scenario 1, the workforce manager has future end strength targets and wants to know how to adjust hiring, so Version 2 of the model is again the appropriate tool for the analysis. However, in this scenario, DoD wants end strength to vary over time. For example,

Figure 4.7
Number of New Hires to Maintain the Current Size of the Civilian AW

	Years of Retirement Eligibility	2011	2012	2013	2014	2015	2016	2017	2018	2019	2020	2021
1	**Model 2: Target End Strength Fixed, New Hire Rate Varies**											
2					Projected Inventory – Base Case							
43	8	721	633	710	840	794	841	828	837	828	843	918
44	9	525	565	496	555	655	619	656	645	652	644	655
45	10	1333	1456	1583	1631	1718	1865	1956	2059	2134	2204	2253
46												
47	Total	135320	135320	135320	135320	135320	135320	135320	135320	135320	135320	135320
48												
49	Target Strength		135320	135320	135320	135320	135320	135320	135320	135320	135320	135320
50	Separations+											
51	Switches		4994	4982	4982	4977	4944	4902	4844	4853	4803	4751
52	New Hires		4994	4982	4982	4977	4944	4902	4844	4853	4803	4751
53	Total Losses		10101	10158	10222	10276	10295	10300	10282	10324	10301	10272
54	Total Gains		10101	10158	10222	10276	10296	10300	10282	10324	10301	10272
55												

suppose DoD wants to grow the civilian workforce by 2,500 workers per year through 2020, then reduce the workforce size by 7,500 between 2020 and 2021. To determine how many new hires are required to meet these targets, the workforce manager would enter the target end strengths into row 49 of the model (Figure 4.8).

The model indicates that approximately 7,500 new hires are required to meet growth targets during the years when the workforce is expected to grow by 2,500 per year. That is, the number of new hires is nearly three times the desired workforce growth. In addition, we see that it is not possible to reach the goal of reducing the workforce by 7,500 between 2020 and 2021 simply by reducing hiring. Even with zero new hires, the resultant workforce will exceed the target. Other strategies, such as layoffs, would be needed to achieve the workforce targets in that year. In response to such a projection, managers might want to consider modifying the (hypothetical) targets to avoid the need for such a dramatic one-year decline in the size of the workforce.

Scenario 3

DoD suspects that separation rates may increase as the economy improves and wants to know how this may affect the civilian AW population.

This scenario requires the workforce manager to examine the implications of changes to separation rates for end strength. Version 1 of the model is the appropriate tool. The projection scenario requires two decisions about model inputs—the new hire rate and the separation rate(s). Decisions about the new hire rate are similar to the decision made under the baseline model, with a choice between the five-year historical average and any other plausible new hire rates the informed manager may choose as an estimate. For the purposes of this scenario, assume a constant new hire rate of 4 percent. The manager would input this value into the "Base Model—FERS" spreadsheet in cell Q23.

After determining a rate for new hires, estimates of the increased separation rates must be input into the "Base Rates—FERS" and "Base Rates—CSRS" sheets. The manager can change the separation rates for any or all of the YORE bins. The manager may reasonably

Figure 4.8
Number of New Hires Under Varying Targets for Civilian AW Size

	Years of Retirement Eligibility	2011	2012	2013	2014	2015	2016	2017	2018	2019	2020	2021
1	**Model 2: Target End Strength Fixed, New Hire Rate Varies**											
2					Projected Inventory - Base Case							
43	8	721	633	711	841	795	844	831	842	834	852	929
44	9	525	565	496	556	656	621	658	648	656	649	662
45	10	1333	1456	1584	1632	1720	1868	1960	2065	2142	2214	2271
46												
47	Total	135320	137820	140320	142820	145320	147820	150320	152820	155320	157820	152655
48												
49	Target Stength		137820	140320	142820	145320	147820	150320	152820	155320	157820	150320
50	Separations+											
51	Switches		4994	5023	5064	5102	5110	5116	5105	5164	5165	5165
52	New Hires		7494	7523	7564	7602	7610	7616	7605	7664	7665	0
53	Total Losses		10101	10303	10512	10713	10878	11034	11167	11363	11495	11623
54	Total Gains		12601	12803	13013	13213	13378	13535	13667	13863	13995	6457
55												

RAND *RR110-4.8*

suspect that the economic recovery will influence employee decisions differently, depending on the employees' proximity to retirement and their retirement plans. For example, a recovery may lead to a larger proportional increase in the separation rate of younger workers, who have a large (and growing) set of alternative employment possibilities, as well as older workers, who see the value of their retirement packages rebound. However, CSRS retirees are likely to see smaller changes in retirement wealth with changes in the economy, so these older workers may have smaller changes in separation rates relative to FERS employees who are retirement eligible. Given these considerations, assume that the manager expects the following changes to separation rates: a 25-percent increase in separation rates for all workers with YORE of –20 or less, a 25-percent increase in separation rates for workers with YORE of 0 or higher in FERS, and a 10-percent increase in separation rates for workers with YORE of 0 or higher in CSRS.[3] This will require the workforce manager to calculate this new set of separation rates and enter them into column C of the "Base Rates—FERS" and "Base Rates—CSRS" spreadsheets, as shown in Figure 4.9.

Figure 4.1 indicated that, with a new hire rate of 4 percent, the size of the civilian AW population is expected to *increase* by approximately 5,500 between 2011 and 2021. Figure 4.10 shows the change in the workforce projections for this scenario of increased separations for younger and older workers. Rather than seeing an increase in the civilian AW population, a

Figure 4.9
Change in Separation Rates from Base Model to "Improved Economy" Scenario

	A	B	C	D	E	F	G	H	I	J	K	L	M
2	FERS Attrition Rates based on Historical Data												
3	Years of Retirement Eligibility	Switch Out Rates (Average)	Separation Rates (Average)	2011	2012	2013	2014	2015	2016	2017	2018	2019	2020
4	-36	0.02167	0.13897	0.839	0.839	0.839	0.839	0.839	0.839	0.839	0.839	0.839	0.839
5	-35	0.01622	0.09773	0.886	0.886	0.886	0.886	0.886	0.886	0.886	0.886	0.886	0.886
6	-34	0.00447	0.05351	0.942	0.942	0.942	0.942	0.942	0.942	0.942	0.942	0.942	0.942
37	-3	0.02788	0.03518	0.937	0.937	0.937	0.937	0.937	0.937	0.937	0.937	0.937	0.937
38	-2	0.02363	0.03219	0.944	0.944	0.944	0.944	0.944	0.944	0.944	0.944	0.944	0.944
39	-1	0.02549	0.03848	0.936	0.936	0.936	0.936	0.936	0.936	0.936	0.936	0.936	0.936
40	0	0.02152	0.13085	0.848	0.848	0.848	0.848	0.848	0.848	0.848	0.848	0.848	0.848
41	1	0.02217	0.1132	0.865	0.865	0.865	0.865	0.865	0.865	0.865	0.865	0.865	0.865
42	2	0.02478	0.1403	0.835	0.835	0.835	0.835	0.835	0.835	0.835	0.835	0.835	0.835
43	3	0.01709	0.15443	0.828	0.828	0.828	0.828	0.828	0.828	0.828	0.828	0.828	0.828
	A	B	C	D	E	F	G	H	I	J	K	L	M
2	FERS Attrition Rates under Improved Economy Assumptions												
3	Years of Retirement Eligibility	Switch Out Rates (Average)	Separation Rates (Average)	2011	2012	2013	2014	2015	2016	2017	2018	2019	2020
4	-36	0.02167	0.17371	0.805	0.805	0.805	0.805	0.805	0.805	0.805	0.805	0.805	0.805
5	-35	0.01622	0.12216	0.862	0.862	0.862	0.862	0.862	0.862	0.862	0.862	0.862	0.862
6	-34	0.00447	0.06689	0.929	0.929	0.929	0.929	0.929	0.929	0.929	0.929	0.929	0.929
37	-3	0.02788	0.03518	0.937	0.937	0.937	0.937	0.937	0.937	0.937	0.937	0.937	0.937
38	-2	0.02363	0.03219	0.944	0.944	0.944	0.944	0.944	0.944	0.944	0.944	0.944	0.944
39	-1	0.02549	0.03848	0.936	0.936	0.936	0.936	0.936	0.936	0.936	0.936	0.936	0.936
40	0	0.02152	0.16356	0.815	0.815	0.815	0.815	0.815	0.815	0.815	0.815	0.815	0.815
41	1	0.02217	0.1415	0.836	0.836	0.836	0.836	0.836	0.836	0.836	0.836	0.836	0.836
42	2	0.02478	0.17538	0.800	0.800	0.800	0.800	0.800	0.800	0.800	0.800	0.800	0.800
43	3	0.01709	0.19303	0.790	0.790	0.790	0.790	0.790	0.790	0.790	0.790	0.790	0.790

---

[3] One possibility for estimating changes in separation rates under economic changes would be to use historical data to examine the changes in separation rates after previous recessions (e.g., 1990–1991, 2001).

Figure 4.10
Civilian AW Projections Under Scenarios with Increased Separations

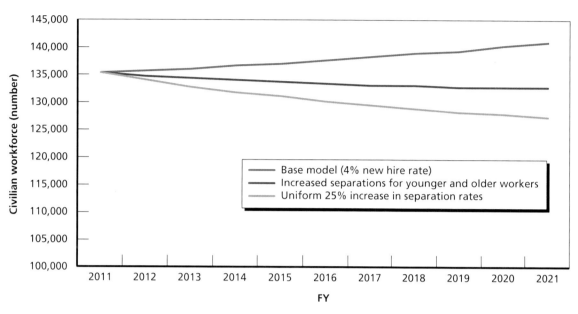

4-percent new hire rate now results in a small *decrease* of approximately 3,000 over the ten-year period. We also include a projection for the civilian population under an assumption of 25-percent increases in separations across the board. This version of the scenario results in a somewhat larger decrease, of more than 8,000 workers, between 2011 and 2021. Given these findings, a workforce manager may want to closely monitor separation trends and be prepared to increase hiring or bring workers in from non-AW positions as needed to address increased separation rates and maintain the size of the workforce.

Scenario 4

The civilian AW target size is 145,000 by 2015, but DoD is not confident that it can achieve a new hire rate greater than 3 percent. The workforce manager wants to explore how much internal hiring (of current non-AW DoD employees) would be needed to fill the gap.

We used Version 1 of the model to examine this scenario. In the current projection model, the rate of recategorization into the AW is held constant across years, and these rates for recategorization must be entered separately for CSRS and FERS retirees on the "Base Model—CSRS" and "Base Model—FERS" spreadsheets, near the new hire rate entry cell (see Figure 4.11). By using a trial-and-error method to gradually increase the switch-in rate, the manager can find the general range of values that will allow the workforce to meet its target of 145,000 by 2015.

It is unlikely that managers will recruit CSRS and FERS individuals differently for recategorization into the AW (within a given YORE cohort), so it is reasonable to assume that the rates of recategorization into the civilian AW are increased at the same rate. Figure 4.12 presents the workforce numbers with recategorizations increased by 75 percent, to 2.6 percent for CSRS employees and 7.3 percent for FERS employees. This rate of increase far exceeds the target of 145,000 civilian AW employees by 2015. In fact, somewhat smaller increases in

Figure 4.11
Changing the Fixed Rate of Recategorization into the AW from Non-AW DoD

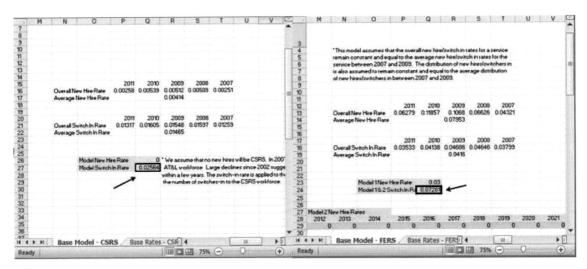

RAND RR110-4.11

Figure 4.12
Workforce Projections with a 75-Percent Increase in Recategorizations into the AW

Model 1: New Hires=Fixed % of Total Population, End Strength Varies

Projected Inventory – Base Case

	Years of Retirement Eligibility	2011	2012	2013	2014	2015	2016	2017	2018	2019	2020	2021
35	0	4020	4111	4461	4900	4667	4786	4651	5149	4797	4649	4769
36	1	3371	3348	3438	3756	4160	3980	4114	4016	4446	4157	4037
37	2	2799	2859	2855	2941	3230	3599	3455	3593	3519	3897	3652
38	3	2400	2386	2435	2431	2502	2743	3052	2932	3048	2988	3304
39	4	1899	2029	2017	2057	2053	2111	2311	2568	2469	2565	2515
40	5	1648	1568	1672	1661	1693	1689	1736	1897	2105	2025	2103
41	6	1121	1332	1268	1351	1341	1366	1363	1401	1531	1697	1633
42	7	798	899	1066	1015	1081	1073	1093	1091	1121	1225	1359
43	8	721	636	716	850	810	864	858	875	877	903	992
44	9	525	568	501	563	666	635	676	671	684	685	705
45	10	1333	1460	1592	1645	1738	1892	1992	2107	2196	2281	2355
46												
47	Total	135320	138214	141277	144503	147898	151492	155299	159336	163539	167970	172632
48												
49	YORE –21 and	26.1%	26.2%	26.3%	26.1%	25.9%	25.6%	25.3%	25.0%	24.7%	24.6%	24.5%
50	YORE –11 to -2	23.0%	23.1%	23.4%	23.8%	24.5%	25.3%	26.1%	26.8%	27.3%	27.7%	28.1%
51	YORE –6 to 10	17.7%	17.3%	16.5%	16.2%	16.1%	15.8%	15.8%	15.8%	15.9%	16.1%	16.2%
52	YORE –1 to –5	18.0%	18.0%	18.3%	17.8%	17.3%	16.9%	16.5%	15.9%	15.7%	15.5%	15.3%
53	YORE 0 to 4	10.7%	10.7%	10.8%	11.1%	11.2%	11.4%	11.3%	11.5%	11.2%	10.9%	10.6%
54	YORE 5 and m	4.5%	4.7%	4.8%	4.9%	5.0%	5.0%	5.0%	5.0%	5.2%	5.2%	5.3%
55												
56												
57	% Eligible for											
58	Retirement	15.2%	15.3%	15.6%	16.0%	16.2%	16.3%	16.3%	16.5%	16.4%	16.1%	15.9%

Full Retirement Model / Base Model - CSRS / Base Rates -

RAND RR110-4.12

recategorizations of 65 percent also meet the target for 2015 (approximately 3,500 additional non-AW employees switching in each year). Using trial and error, a workforce manager could find the exact number of additional recategorizations necessary to exactly meet the population target.

Tips for Manipulating the Projection Models

The above examples are intended to illustrate the way the projection workbooks can be used to help managers explore the workforce implications of a wide variety of changes and go beyond the default assumptions used in the model. We recommend that, when manipulating the model parameters, the user immediately save the worksheet under a new name to retain the information contained in the original model. Managers are advised to make use of their expert judgment and historical data obtained from other sources to adjust the underlying rates used in the model. Finally, we recommend that managers focus on manipulating only one variable at a time to understand how each aspect of the model affects workforce projections.

CHAPTER FIVE

The Military Acquisition Workforce and Its Implications for the Civilian Acquisition Workforce

This chapter presents insights on the military AW based on our analysis of DoD data. The first section provides a descriptive overview of the military AW. The second section describes the relationship between the military and civilian workforces and how it varies by service. The third section discusses the military AW as a source of new hires into the civilian AW.

We have made two refinements to the analysis of the military workforce over Gates et al., 2008. These changes are due largely to several years of experience with the military WEX data. First, we adjusted measurement of several career descriptors, such as length of service in the military and most recent service, to be relative to the reporting period. Second, we corrected a programming error that led to the undercounting of the military AW in some years.

Military Personnel Are a Minority in the Acquisition Workforce

In parallel to the civilian AW, members of the military are also coded as being in the AW. Figure 5.1 shows the time trajectory for the number of military members in the AW. Figure 5.1 and other data presented in this section are from the WEX file, linked to the DAWIA data. The military AW total was 15,411 in FY 2011.

Historically, the military AW has been roughly an order of magnitude smaller than the civilian AW (see Figure 3.1). The size of the military AW has varied more modestly than that of the civilian AW.

Military Acquisition Workforce Representation Highest in Air Force

The previous section indicates that, while the AW includes both military and civilian personnel, military personnel are a distinct minority. The share of a service's AW workforce that consists of military personnel varies by service, suggesting that services make different choices about how and when to use military personnel in acquisition roles.

Figure 5.2 displays civilian and military totals by service. In terms of absolute numbers, military personnel are most prominent in the Air Force. The share of the AW that is military is significantly larger than the shares for the Army and the Navy.

As Figure 5.3 shows, about 85 percent of military personnel in the AW are officers, in near-symmetrical contrast to the less than 15 percent of military personnel, overall, who are officers.

Figure 5.1
Military Acquisition Workforce Size by Fiscal Year, September 30 Annual Snapshots

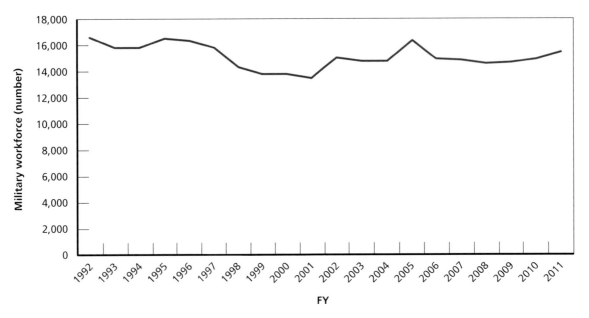

RAND *RR110-5.1*

Figure 5.2
Total Civilian and Military Acquisition Workers, by Service, FY 2011

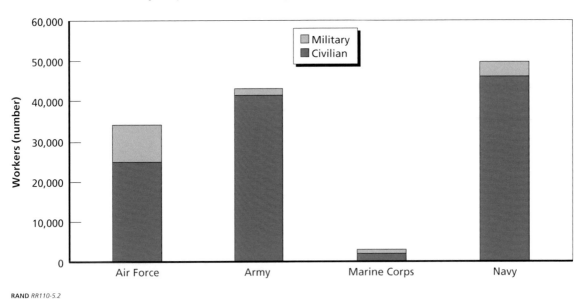

RAND *RR110-5.2*

The Workforce Is Not Spread Out Evenly Throughout Career Fields

In Chapter Three, we presented information on the career field distribution of the civilian AW (Figure 3.5). We noted that the largest civilians career fields by far are systems planning, research, development, and engineering and contracting and that only 8 percent of civilian acquisition employees are in program management. Figure 5.4 presents information on the acquisition career field for the military AW in FY 2011. The largest share of military acquisi-

Figure 5.3
Enlistment Status of Military AW and All Military Personnel, FY 2011

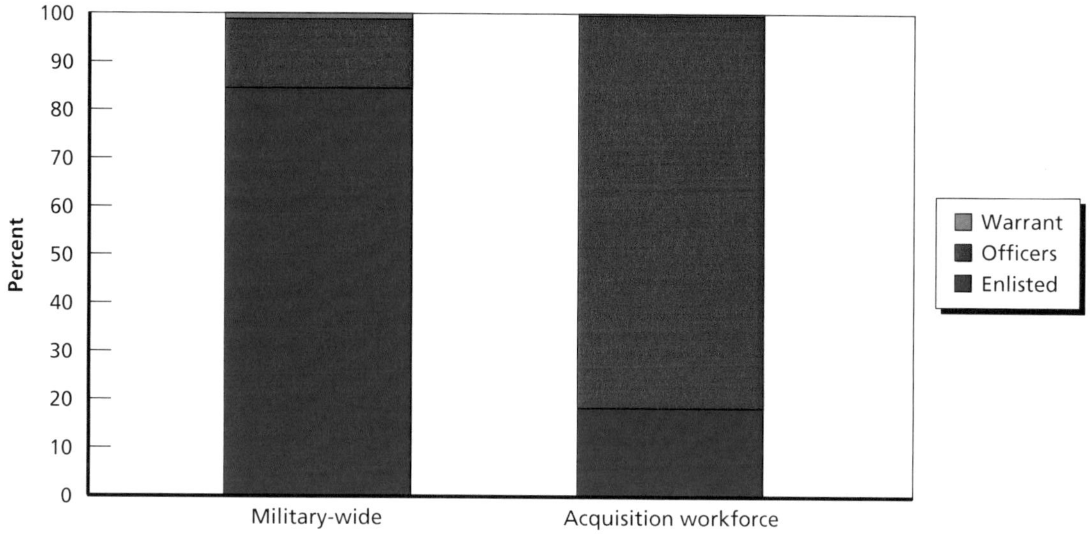

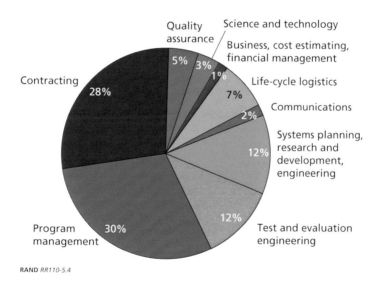

RAND *RR110-5.3*

Figure 5.4
Career Field Distribution for the Military AW, FY 2011

RAND *RR110-5.4*

tion workers are in the program management career field (30 percent of the total), followed by contracting, with 28 percent of the total. In contrast, a number of career fields had few or no military personnel: auditing, science and technology, manufacturing and production, purchasing and procurement, and industrial property management.

Highly Experienced Military Personnel Constitute a Large Share of New AW Hires

Military members of the AW are of particular interest to us because we suspect they are prominent candidates to leave the military and become leaders of the civilian AW. We cannot say with complete confidence what fraction of current AW civilian employees had prior military experience. Military experience flags in the civilian inventory file appear to be unreliable. As noted previously, our WEX data go back only to 1975. We know that numerous senior DoD civilian employees served in the military during the Vietnam era or earlier but were not able to identify these individuals using our data.

We have greater confidence, however, in our ability to calibrate the level of military experience among new civilian hires. As discussed in Chapter Two, the only new hires whose military experience we could not tabulate would be those who left the military before 1975. Although there are doubtlessly some, we do not think there are many new civilian employees hired in 1992 or later whose military service ended before 1975.

As shown in Figure 5.5, there has been a marked and interesting trend in both DoD-wide and AW rates of military experience of new civilian hires.

In FY 2011, 41 percent of new AW and over 56 percent of new DoD civilian employees had prior military experience. Both figures represent significant increases over the share of new hires with prior military experience in FY 1992 (31 percent for DoD as a whole and 24 percent for the AW). In every year since 1993, the percentage of new hires into the AW with prior military experience has been lower than for DoD as a whole. The percentage of new hires with prior military experience into the AW did decline slightly between FY 2007 and FY 2009, coincident with a rise in the number of new hires into the AW in support of the AW growth initiative.

There is no single explanation for this general upward trend in the share of new hires with prior military experience. A number of factors may play a role. Military-civilian conversions may have encouraged hiring civilians with military experience—often the very individuals who previously performed the function as members of the military—during the late 1990s. An October 1999 policy change that removed an income cap that had discouraged higher-ranking military retirees from taking federal jobs may have played a role in the continued increase after

Figure 5.5
The Rate of Military Experience Among New Civilian Hires

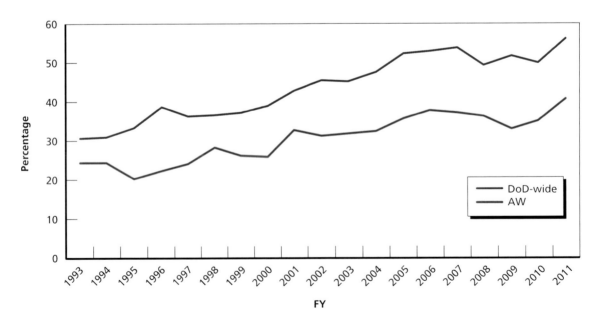

1999 as the military-civilian conversions began to wind down.[1] Policy priorities to support the hiring of Gulf War veterans may also have played a role after 2001.

Figure 5.6 plots the proportion of new hires with military experience who were high ranking. We defined a military new hire to be *high ranking* if he or she attained a rank of E7 or above, O5 or above, or WO3 or above while in the military. These are the ranks we think would typically correspond to full-career military retirees (of course, there will always be exceptions, e.g., prior enlisted personnel who later become officers and retire as O4s). In the AW, the proportion who were high ranking has grown in recent years, consistent with the theory that the pay cap had been a binding constraint, but we did not observe any change in the percentage of high-ranking new hires DoD-wide (although, as shown in Figure 5.5, there was a marked increase in the proportion of new hires with military experience both in the AW and DoD-wide).

In FY 2011, 44 percent of new hires into the AW with prior military experience were high ranking. For all DoD civilian hires, the figure was 33 percent. Since 1993, the share of high-ranking individuals among the pool of new hires with prior military experience has increased substantially. Between FY 2000 and FY 2001, the share of new hires into the AW with prior military experience who were high ranking increased from 32 percent to 41 percent, again suggesting that the October 1999 removal of the pay cap may have encouraged former military to join the civilian AW.

Figure 5.7 shows the percentage breakdown of prior military service for FY 2011 AW hires with prior military experience. Each bar in the chart represents the new civilian hires into a military service (or other parts of DoD). As reflected in the figure, a vast majority of the

Figure 5.6
Percentage of New Civilian Hires with Military Experience Who Were High-Ranking

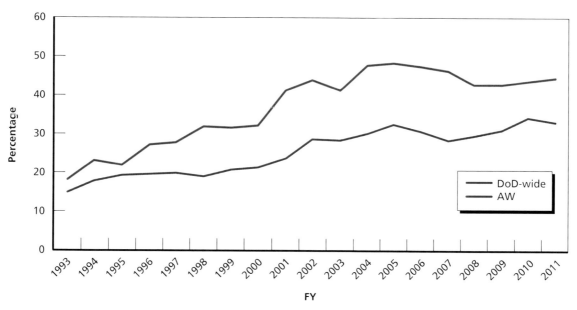

---

[1] Prior to October 1, 1999, a pay cap limited the combined total of federal civilian basic salary plus military retired pay to the Executive Level V compensation level (which was $110,700 at the time).

Figure 5.7
Military Services of New Civilian Acquisition Workforce Hires, by Civilian Hiring Component, 2011

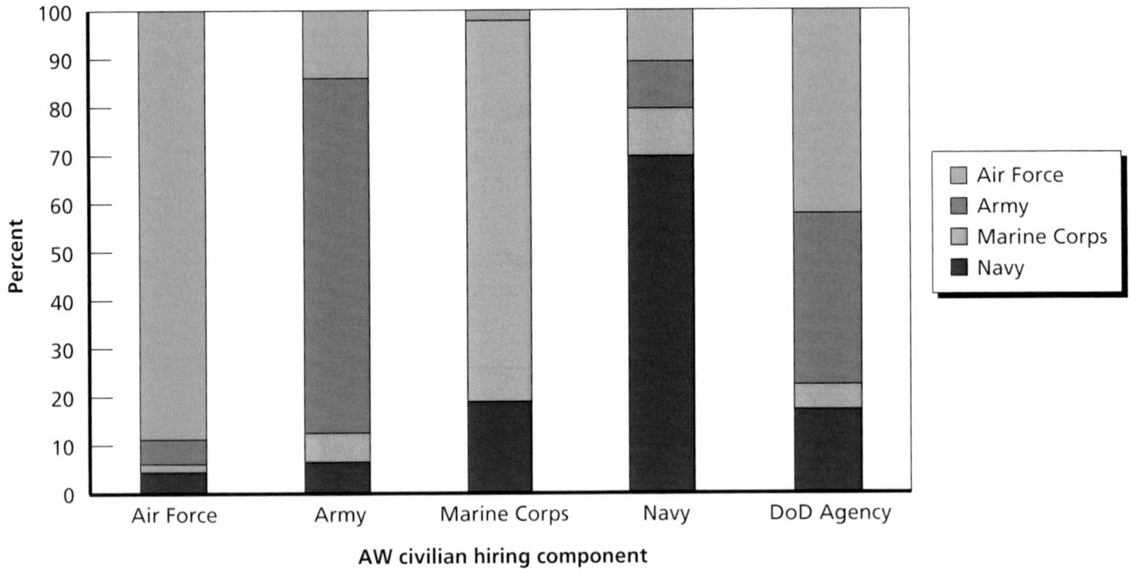

new civilian hires with prior military experience into the Air Force, Army, Marine Corps, and Navy had their military service in the same organization. DoD agencies hire individuals from each of the services.

Although military members represent a minority of the AW overall, they appear to be an important and growing source of future civilian AW leaders. The share of new hires into the AW who have prior military experience has grown dramatically over time, along with the share of those who were high ranking at the time they left the military. Given that 41 percent of new AW hires in FY 2011 had prior military experience, DoD may want to develop a better understanding of how the career trajectories of these individuals compare with the career trajectories of civilian new hires with no military experience.

CHAPTER SIX

Conclusions

The DoD AW supports military readiness and ensures that DoD gets the best value for its contract expenditures. Understanding the makeup of the AW population and tracking changes in the population over time are important to ensure effective management and planning. To support AT&L Human Capital Initiatives efforts to manage and develop strategic plans for the workforce, our analysis documents a number of characteristics of the AW workforce and tracks changes in the population since FY 2006. The report also documents a number of improvements to RAND's AW projection tool.

Findings

Growth in the civilian AW appears to have met the targets set forth by the Secretary of Defense's 2009 AW growth initiative. The growth initiative called for the addition of 20,000 civilian acquisition workers between 2008 and 2015; by 2011, the civilian AW population had grown by 24,571 workers. This growth was driven by substantial increases in populations for all services except the Army. The Army civilian AW population decreased by approximately 2,500 between 2008 and 2011, and the Army share of the civilian AW workforce decreased from 39 percent to 30 percent. There continues to be substantial movement of DoD civilian employees between the AW and non-AW workforces. Our analysis suggests that administrative recategorizations have declined over recent years, so these recategorizations are more likely to be substantive shifts (or "internal hires") of civilian workers into the AW, as opposed to reclassification of positions into the AW. Nevertheless, about one-half of the recategorizations still appear to be administrative, based on the data available to us. These administrative changes remain a challenge for workforce planning.

The attrition rates for the civilian AW, defined as those who leave DoD civilian employment, remain low relative to attrition rates for all DoD civilians. Rates of attrition were at 20-year lows in 2009 and 2010, likely driven by high national unemployment rates and concerns about stock market and pension values. Within these broad trends, there was some variation by segment of the AW. For example, attrition rates are higher for the contracting career field than for the SPRDE career field. The attrition rates for the STEM AW workforce are lower than for the non-STEM AW and are also lower than for the DoD-wide STEM workforce.

It appears that FERS employees leave the workforce at lower rates than CSRS employees both prior to and after retirement eligibility. This differs from our 2008 findings that FERS employees separated at somewhat higher rates prior to eligibility. We hypothesize that this change may be driven by economic conditions that affected the value of retirement packages disproportionately for FERS employees.

The military is a relatively small portion of the AW, accounting for approximately 11 percent of the total. However, the military composition varies by service, with substantially larger shares of the AW in the military for the Air Force and the Marines relative to the Navy and the Army. The military members of the AW are predominately officers, in contrast with the overall military workforce. The distribution of military AW employees also varies by career field, with a significantly larger portion of military employees in program management relative to their civilian counterparts. Despite being a relatively small portion of the AW, military personnel comprise a significant and growing share of new hires. This is also the case DoD-wide. We find that these military new hires are often high ranking, with 44 percent of military new hires having achieved a rank of E7, O5, WO3, or higher during their period of military experience.

When we apply the projection model using five-year historical averages (the default assumptions), the model projects that the civilian AW will grow dramatically over ten years. However, there is ample reason to doubt that the historical average rates will be maintained in the future. In particular, hiring was unusually high in 2009 and 2010 due to the AW growth initiative. As a result, the five-year average may not be a good approximation of hiring and separation rates in future years. When we used a more-modest hiring rate of 4 percent, the projected AW civilian population was relatively stable. More generally, the value of the projection model and resulting projections is not so much in the specific projection values the model provides but in the insights that managers might gain in manipulating the model to examine the possible effects of changes in the underlying data.

Recommendations

This report describes some of the workforce supply analyses of the DoD AW that can be supported by DoD data. Supply analysis is only part of the strategic human capital planning. Supply analyses must ultimately be combined with demand analyses. As defense budgets come under pressure, DoD must ensure that the civilian workforce is structured as efficiently as possible. A more-systematic and data-based understanding of workload drivers for the AW and the relationship between changes in the acquisition process and workload levels would facilitate strategic human capital planning for the AW.

One objective of the AW growth initiative was to increase the size of the organic civilian AW through a combination of insourcing contractor positions and new hiring. As we noted in our 2008 report, DoD-wide information on contractors who are performing acquisition-related functions is lacking. To date, there has been little progress in terms of the development of such data. As a result, we were unable to assess the extent to which insourcing contributed to AW growth. Better information on the contract workforce is critical for managers interested in assessing the health of the AW.

YORE Inventory Projection Model: Technical Details

The YORE inventory projection model described in Chapter Four is a modification of the YOS-based model presented in Gates et al., 2008. We revised the original model to incorporate two important changes. First, the prior inventory projection model was based on information about an employees' YOS, but the new version of the model is based on an individual's YORE, as described in Gates et al., 2008 (pp. 9–10). Second, we added a component to the projection model that allows the user to input a personnel ceiling, above which the personnel projection is not allowed to go, to see how the number of new hires would need to adjust to achieve that goal. The original projection model is now identified as Version 1, and the new component is identified as Version 2.

This appendix describes the Excel notebook containing the projection model, the features of that workbook, and how the workbook calculates projections and offers guidance for users about how to manipulate the model.

Model Overview

Our workforce inventory projection model, shown in Figure A.1, takes as its inputs information on the number of AW employees, rates of accession, rates of separation and rates of recategorization. In our application of the model, workforce counts and turnover rates are calculated for each YORE group. Version 1 is displayed on the left-hand side of the first tab, "Base Retirement Model." Version 2 is displayed on the right side of this tab. The starting point for the projection is the distribution of the AW in FY 2011 by YORE.

Because our prior research revealed that the separation rates for a given YORE cell differ by retirement plan, the YORE projection model separately projects inventories of CSRS and FERS employees and then adds these two projections to provide an overall projection. The model excludes individuals who are part of a retirement plan other than CSRS or FERS. For FY 2011, this analysis excludes 662 individuals in the AW on this basis. Our analysis of these individuals indicates that they are typically employees who are hired on a limited-term basis.

The original YOS projection model described in Gates et al., 2008, included only four tabs: "Base Model," "Base Rates," "Gains Data," and "Losses Data." The YORE version of the model includes nine tabs, some of which are visible in Figure A.1: the original four tabs with separate data for CSRS and FERS, plus a "Full Retirement Model" tab that adds the data from the CSRS and FERS projections to provide a single projection and a summary by YORE:

- Full Retirement Model
- Base Model—CSRS

Figure A.1
Projection Model Overview Snapshot

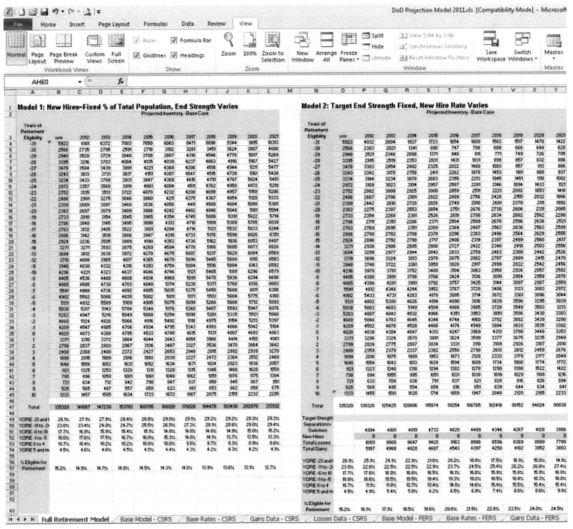

- Base Rates—CSRS
- Gains Data—CSRS
- Losses Data—CSRS
- Base Model—FERS
- Base Rates—FERS
- Gains Data—FERS
- Losses Data—FERS.

To obtain projections for FY 2011, we applied the following procedure to both the FERS and the CSRS Base Models separately. We then rolled up the results in the "Full Retirement Model" sheet to provide an overview for the total workforce.

Procedure for Generating the Projections

The model arrays the base year population according to YORE. To calculate the projection, we first let the employees in each YORE cell "age" by one year: Individuals with YORE –10 in FY 2010 were moved into YORE –9 for FY 2011. We then accounted for the fact that some people might have left the DoD workforce or stayed in DoD but left the AW during this time. To do this, we calculated an expected continuation rate for each YORE bin. In our model, the expected continuation rate is simply 1 minus the average rate of separation from DoD over the past five years minus the average substantive recategorization rate over the past five years for that YORE.

We next applied the five-year average rate of new hires to the total prior-year inventory to calculate the expected total number of new hires between FYs 2011 and 2012. We calculated the historical new hire rate by dividing the total number of new hires (CSRS + FERS) in a given year by the total number of employees in the prior year. We then generated a projection of the number of new hires in the future by multiplying the historical average new hire rate by the total number of employees (CSRS + FERS). The YORE projection model makes a simplifying assumption that all new hires enter into FERS. In FY 2011, there were 59 new hires into CSRS and 8,262 new hires into FERS—less than 1 percent of new hires were in CSRS. This share will continue to decline over time. We then calculated the expected YORE distribution of the new hires using historical averages for the YORE distribution of new FERS hires.

Finally, we calculated the expected number and YORE distribution of substantive switches into the AW between FYs 2011 and 2012 separately for the FERS and CSRS populations based on five-year historical averages.

The next two sections of this appendix provide detailed information on the model and how to use it.

Acquisition Workforce YORE Projection Model Details

This section provides detailed information on the AW inventory projection model. The actual workforce projection model is available from the authors on request as a Microsoft Excel workbook.

Key inputs to the model are beginning inventories by YORE and separation, recategorization (switch in and switch out), and new hire rates.

Basic Configuration of the Model

The basic workforce characteristic depicted in the model is *YORE*. The model accepts as user input the beginning inventory of a workforce, distributed from YORE –31 to YORE 10.[1] The model uses continuation rates to calculate the number of workers in each YORE category who are expected to remain in the workforce for an additional year. These continuation rates take into account expected losses due to separations and losses through substantive (but not administrative) recategorizations (switches out) of the AW. The model uses an overall gain rate, a gain distribution by YORE, and the previous year's end strength to calculate the number of workers

---

[1] YORE 10 contains all workers with ten or fewer years to retirement (YORE from 0 to 10); YORE –31 contains all workers with at least 31 years to retirement (YORE less than –31). See "Technical Notes" for more information about YORE bins.

in each YORE who are expected to enter the workforce.[2] These gain rates and gain distributions are separated into gains due to new hires and gains due to recategorizations (switches in) to the workforce. These calculations are performed separately for the CSRS and FERS populations and then rolled up to provide an aggregate projection. In summary, the model starts with a workforce as it looks at the end of FY 2011 and depicts how it might look at the end of each successive FY, assuming average historical gains and losses apply in the future.[3]

Figure A.2 illustrates the basic configuration of the overall model for Version 1, which projects the future workforce size based on average historical gain and loss dynamics. Column A of the "Full Retirement Model" sheet indicates the YORE. Column B contains the beginning inventory as it looked at the end of FY 2011.[4] Columns C through L contain the projected workforce at the ends of FYs 2012 through 2021. As with the original version of the model, the user can adjust new hire rates and switch-in rates. These adjustments must be done separately for the CSRS and FERS populations (if desired and as needed). For example, to adjust the assumed new hire rate for FERS employees, the user would go to the "Base Model— FERS" tab and adjust the rate that is driving the FERS projection in cell Q23. Currently, the model uses the five-year historical average rates as default for everything except the CSRS new hire rate, which is assumed to be zero.

Related information about the CSRS and FERS workforces is summarized separately in the sheets labeled "Base Model—CSRS" and "Base Model—FERS." The underlying rates are in the sheet labeled "Base Rates—CSRS" and "Base Rates—FERS."

Row 47 indicates the expected end strength for future FYs. Rows 49–58 describe how the projected future workforce would be distributed across YORE blocks and the total share of the workforce eligible for retirement in a given year.

Projection Model Version 2: User Fixes Target End Strength

Version 2 allows the user to input a target end strength and then automatically varies the new hire rate to achieve or at least approach that target end strength. Separation rates, and recategorization rates are assumed to be held constant. Figure A.3 depicts the model. This version of the model is found starting in column N of the first tab "Full Retirement Model." Version 2 allows the user to specify target end strengths in the yellow highlighted row (row 49). The model assumes that loss rates (separations and switches out) and substantive switch-in rates are consistent with historical averages.[5] The model outputs (orange-highlighted row, 52) the number of new hires that one would need to meet that workforce target holding all else equal. Row 53 provides the total losses that would be expected in that year (due to separation and switches out), and row 54 provides the total number of gains (from new hires and from

---

[2] An alternative version of this model requires the user to input end strengths and calculate the number of new hires necessary to achieve this desired end strength. This model differs by requiring the user to input new-hire and switch-in rates and calculate the end strengths that result.

[3] To be precise, these are the new hires or switchers-in who last until the end of the FY in which they were hired or switched in. We do not observe in the data individuals who were hired in the course of an FY and quit before the end of that FY. If such short-term turnover were prevalent, the number of people DoD would need to hire to achieve the number of new hires, as we have defined it here, would be higher.

[4] The data used in this example reflect the beginning inventory embedded in the workbook when it is initially supplied to users. This beginning inventory depicts the DoD-wide AW according to the acquisition flags included in the DoD Civilian Inventory File from DMDC.

[5] Model 2 does not allow users to manually adjust gain and loss rates.

Figure A.2
Basic Configuration for Version 1

Model 1: New Hires=Fixed % of Total Population, End Strength Varies

Projected Inventory – Base Case

Years of Retirement Eligibility	2011	2012	2013	2014	2015	2016	2017	2018	2019	2020	2021
-31	5323	6101	6372	7003	7650	8063	8471	8896	9344	9815	10313
-30	2566	2735	2795	2591	2718	3102	3281	3451	3624	3807	4000
-29	2940	3520	3729	3840	3708	3887	4310	4546	4778	5017	5269
-28	3395	3216	3783	4004	4135	4039	4237	4663	4916	5167	5427
-27	3478	3584	3439	3991	4221	4368	4306	4518	4944	5211	5477
-26	3243	3613	3731	3617	4151	4387	4547	4515	4738	5161	5438
-25	3234	3433	3799	3931	3847	4369	4615	4791	4787	5024	5451
-24	2972	3357	3560	3919	4061	4004	4511	4762	4950	4972	5219
-23	2752	3135	3513	3722	4078	4232	4200	4698	4957	5158	5206
-22	2486	2901	3275	3646	3860	4211	4375	4367	4854	5120	5333
-21	2309	2689	3097	3468	3836	4058	4411	4588	4604	5088	5365
-20	2363	2697	3079	3489	3866	4242	4482	4846	5048	5101	5594
-19	2733	2810	3154	3545	3965	4354	4745	5008	5391	5622	5714
-18	2786	3048	3145	3495	3890	4313	4710	5109	5389	5785	6039
-17	2763	3132	3405	3522	3881	4284	4714	5121	5532	5833	6244
-16	2886	3142	3519	3806	3947	4318	4733	5176	5598	6026	6351
-15	2924	3236	3505	3889	4190	4353	4736	5162	5616	6053	6497
-14	3271	3271	3593	3875	4269	4584	4770	5166	5605	6073	6526
-13	3684	3612	3638	3972	4270	4675	5007	5217	5629	6084	6569
-12	3719	4008	3965	4017	4365	4678	5096	5445	5680	6110	6583
-11	3948	4030	4332	4316	4393	4754	5084	5516	5884	6143	6592
-10	4296	4221	4323	4637	4646	4746	5121	5465	5911	6296	6579
-9	4405	4536	4488	4608	4934	4968	5091	5478	5836	6294	6696
-8	4865	4585	4730	4703	4840	5174	5230	5371	5768	6136	6603
-7	5541	4988	4736	4892	4885	5035	5375	5450	5608	6011	6386
-6	4902	5582	5066	4838	5002	5011	5171	5513	5604	5775	6180
-5	5131	4932	5589	5109	4905	5075	5098	5266	5608	5712	5893
-4	5038	5317	5143	5784	5348	5176	5360	5407	5593	5947	6076
-3	5263	4947	5210	5049	5660	5254	5098	5281	5335	5521	5866
-2	4660	5124	4826	5066	4916	5492	5116	4975	5154	5213	5397
-1	4209	4547	4985	4706	4934	4795	5343	4993	4866	5042	5104
0	4020	4073	4388	4795	4533	4745	4615	5131	4807	4693	4863
1	3371	3310	3372	3664	4044	3843	4058	3966	4414	4150	4061
2	2799	2837	2803	2867	3136	3487	3327	3536	3470	3864	3642
3	2400	2368	2400	2372	2427	2653	2948	2815	2992	2939	3270
4	1899	2015	1989	2016	1993	2039	2227	2472	2364	2512	2469
5	1648	1558	1652	1631	1652	1634	1671	1824	2023	1936	2057
6	1121	1325	1253	1328	1311	1328	1315	1345	1468	1628	1559
7	798	896	1058	1001	1061	1048	1062	1051	1076	1175	1304
8	721	634	712	842	798	847	837	850	845	867	951
9	525	565	497	557	658	623	661	653	662	658	675
10	1333	1457	1585	1634	1723	1872	1967	2075	2155	2232	2295
Total	135320	141087	147230	153761	160705	168120	176028	184478	193430	202970	213132
YORE -21 and	26.1%	27.1%	27.9%	28.4%	28.8%	29.0%	29.1%	29.2%	29.2%	29.3%	29.3%
YORE -11 to -2	23.0%	23.4%	24.0%	24.7%	25.5%	26.5%	27.3%	28.1%	28.6%	29.0%	29.4%
YORE -6 to 10	17.7%	16.9%	15.9%	15.4%	15.1%	14.8%	14.8%	14.8%	14.9%	15.0%	15.2%
YORE -1 to -5	18.0%	17.6%	17.5%	16.7%	16.0%	15.3%	14.8%	14.1%	13.7%	13.5%	13.3%
YORE 0 to 4	10.7%	10.4%	10.2%	10.2%	10.0%	10.0%	9.8%	9.7%	9.3%	8.9%	8.6%
YORE 5 and m	4.5%	4.6%	4.6%	4.5%	4.5%	4.4%	4.3%	4.2%	4.3%	4.2%	4.1%
% Eligible for Retirement	15.2%	14.9%	14.7%	14.8%	14.5%	14.3%	14.0%	13.9%	13.6%	13.1%	12.7%

Full Retirement Model / Base Model - CSRS / Base Rates - CSRS / Gains Data - CSRS

RAND RR110-A.2

switches in). The difference in the size of the inventory between one year and the next is equal to the difference between total gains and total losses. The model adjusts the number of new hires to reach the target end strength. In the event that the target strength is lower than what

Figure A.3
Basic Configuration for Version 2

Model 2: Target End Strength Fixed, New Hire Rate Varies

Projected Inventory - Base Case

Years of Retirement Eligibility	2011	2012	2013	2014	2015	2016	2017	2018	2019	2020	2021
-31	5923	4450	4359	4708	5205	5499	5600	5668	5738	5802	4408
-30	2566	2454	2346	1956	1830	2037	2242	2297	2329	2358	2137
-29	2940	2723	3106	3016	2660	2549	2745	2940	3000	3035	2364
-28	3395	2976	2919	3286	3209	2882	2784	2973	3163	3224	3049
-27	3478	3360	3107	3061	3410	3343	3045	2958	3140	3321	3185
-26	3243	3397	3419	3190	3153	3481	3424	3150	3075	3247	3228
-25	3234	3202	3487	3514	3305	3275	3586	3536	3285	3217	3179
-24	2972	3159	3250	3520	3551	3361	3337	3629	3586	3357	3123
-23	2752	2933	3232	3323	3580	3613	3438	3419	3697	3660	3270
-22	2486	2714	2997	3281	3370	3615	3648	3489	3475	3737	3542
-21	2309	2492	2827	3099	3370	3459	3693	3727	3582	3572	3649
-20	2363	2360	2738	3059	3319	3579	3666	3889	3927	3793	3491
-19	2733	2446	2666	3031	3341	3593	3843	3928	4145	4185	3742
-18	2786	2779	2673	2887	3238	3536	3779	4019	4106	4315	4119
-17	2763	2842	3013	2919	3128	3466	3752	3986	4219	4305	4252
-16	2886	2853	3105	3275	3194	3399	3724	4002	4230	4456	4288
-15	2924	2965	3099	3346	3515	3444	3644	3958	4228	4449	4430
-14	3271	3005	3207	3342	3584	3751	3690	3885	4190	4451	4432
-13	3684	3362	3261	3462	3598	3837	4002	3949	4143	4440	4474
-12	3719	3759	3603	3515	3715	3853	4086	4251	4207	4397	4467
-11	3948	3805	3981	3840	3763	3962	4099	4330	4494	4458	4448
-10	4296	4027	4008	4185	4056	3989	4187	4324	4552	4716	4515
-9	4405	4348	4205	4194	4372	4256	4197	4392	4529	4753	4750
-8	4865	4426	4467	4337	4334	4509	4403	4353	4545	4679	4759
-7	5541	4847	4511	4556	4437	4439	4611	4514	4470	4658	4664
-6	4902	5463	4870	4552	4599	4488	4493	4660	4571	4533	4611
-5	5131	4828	5421	4859	4559	4606	4503	4510	4673	4591	4465
-4	5038	5066	4926	5491	4959	4675	4722	4625	4636	4792	4496
-3	5263	4899	4946	4811	5344	4841	4573	4618	4528	4539	4646
-2	4660	5078	4755	4788	4657	5154	4681	4429	4471	4387	4358
-1	4209	4511	4921	4615	4642	4517	4985	4538	4300	4340	4229
0	4020	4045	4338	4716	4425	4446	4326	4762	4342	4119	4131
1	3371	3299	3340	3612	3966	3737	3788	3702	4080	3731	3537
2	2799	2827	2787	2832	3082	3409	3224	3289	3225	3557	3251
3	2400	2361	2387	2354	2391	2600	2874	2719	2775	2722	2993
4	1899	2011	1980	2001	1974	2005	2177	2404	2276	2322	2274
5	1648	1555	1647	1621	1638	1615	1639	1779	1963	1859	1894
6	1121	1324	1250	1323	1302	1315	1297	1317	1429	1577	1493
7	798	895	1056	998	1056	1039	1050	1036	1052	1142	1260
8	721	633	710	840	794	842	829	839	831	846	922
9	525	565	496	555	656	620	656	646	653	647	658
10	1333	1456	1583	1631	1719	1866	1957	2062	2138	2209	2264
Total	135320	132500	135000	137500	140000	142500	145000	147500	150000	152500	147447
Target Stength	130000	132500	135000	137500	140000	142500	145000	147500	150000	152500	145000
Separations+ Switches		4994	4936	4976	5012	5021	5015	5005	5058	5057	5053
New Hires		2174	7436	7476	7512	7521	7515	7505	7558	7557	0
Total Losses		10101	9994	10202	10402	10567	10712	10846	11036	11166	11288
Total Gains		7281	12495	12703	12902	13068	13212	13346	13536	13666	6236

Full Retirement Model / Base Model - CSRS / Base Rates - CSRS / Gains Data - CSRS / Losses Data - CSRS

RAND RR110-A.3

would be achieved with zero new hires, the number of new hires is set to zero and the projected strength will exceed the target end strength.

This alternative model provides users with a way to think about how hiring targets should be adjusted to achieve workforce size goals assuming separation rates and switch rates remain the same. Clearly, policymakers could also consider adjusting continuation rates concurrently with adjustments to hiring policies.

Technical Notes

This section provides additional information about elements of the Excel workbook.

YORE Bins

In an inventory matrix, the bins identify the population with n years relative to retirement eligibility. Thus, YORE 0 identifies the population who will become eligible for retirement within the next FY (i.e., they are not yet eligible as of the end of the current FY but will become eligible within the next FY). We expect to see a lot of these people retire before the end of the next FY. YORE −1 identifies the population with at least one full FY ahead of them before they reach full retirement eligibility. YORE +1 identifies the people who became retirement eligible in a given FY and remained in the workforce through the end of that FY.

The "Base Rates—FERS" and "Base Rates—CSRS" tabs describe continuation rates for each YORE bin. The continuation rate for a particular YORE indicates the proportion of these workers who are expected to survive into the next FY. Default continuation rates are calculated as 1 minus the average separation rate for workers with YORE over five years minus the average switching-out rate over five years.[6] However, the user of the model may choose to modify the continuation rates for particular YORE bins and particular years by changing one or more of the highlighted yellow cells from columns D through M. The user might want to modify the continuation rate to account for expected changes in future retention patterns. For example, if an organization was planning to offer early retirement incentives for individuals who are not yet retirement eligible but will be reaching eligibility within the next five years, the organization may want to reduce the continuation rate for YORE bins −5 to −1 for the years when these incentives are planned.

Gains in the FERS workforce (both new hires and switches in) are distributed across YORE bins according to historical averages by default. These rates are presented in the "Base Rates—FERS" tab, starting at Row 63. The user can choose to change these distributions, so long as the distributions across YORE bins for a given year add up to 1. A user may wish to change these defaults if the organization is planning a shift in its hiring strategy, for example to target more midcareer personnel. Gains to the CSRS workforce are treated differently because very few new hires are part of CSRS. The gain rates used in the model are presented on "Base Rates—CSRS" tab, starting at row 43. The model assumes that no new hires are in CSRS, and the hiring gain distribution includes 0s for all YORE bins. The model does allow switches into the CSRS workforce. These are based on historical averages, but the model does start zeroing out switches in at the lower YORE range for CSRS employees in future years. As with the FERS distributions, the user can choose to change these rates.

Survivors from FY 2011 Strength

The calculations used here are made by compounding the continuation rates along a diagonal in the continuation rate matrix; multiplying the compound, multiyear continuation rate by the appropriate YORE bin in the FY 2011 beginning inventory; and summing the products.

---

[6] The separation and switch-out rates by year are provided on the "Losses Data—FERS" and "Losses Data—CSRS" tabs. We include substantive but not administrative switches out of the AW.

Considerations in Applying the Model to Subsets of the AW

When applying the model to subsets of the AW, such as AW career fields or specific DoD agencies, one must keep in mind the differences in how gains and losses are being considered for these populations. In projecting the future size of a subset of the population, say an AW career field, we need to account for people not only leaving DoD or the AW but also potentially leaving the career field but still remaining in the AW. A person who switches career fields within the AW is a gain to one career field and a loss to another. These dynamics are captured in the context of the population-specific models.

For the career field projections, we *do* count switches between AW career fields as substantive switches in or out of the career field, even though these people are not moving into or out of the AW. So, for example, someone in the program management career field who moves to contracting would be counted as a substantive switch out of program management and a switch into contracting. Similarly, looking at the Army AW, we count someone as a switch if they moved into the Army from a different service or agency even if they were in the AW in both periods. There will be more switching in and out in the subpopulations of the AW than there is switching into and out of the AW.

To apply the projection model to smaller populations, such as small career fields or defense agencies, some modifications are needed to address the fact that continuation or separation rates for any one YORE cell may be highly variable or even nonexistent in some years. Because of this variability, it is often not advisable to use five-year averages for individual YORE cells from some smaller subpopulations. For such populations, we generate an alternative version of the model in which we average the YORE-specific continuation rates across five YORE groupings and use these average rates as inputs to the projection model. Specifically, rather than use a different continuation rate (1 minus the separation rate minus the switch-out rate) for YORE 0, 1, 2, 3, 4, etc., we apply the average separation rate for individuals in YORE 0–4, YORE 5–9, etc. Averaging in this way helps avoid idiosyncratic problems due to a low number of observations in any one YORE cell.

Manipulating the Inventory Projection Model

The real value of the inventory projection model is not so much in the specific projection values it provides but in the insights that managers might gain in manipulating it to examine the possible effect of changes to the underlying data. The workbook contains a beginning inventory for the AW of the population of interest equal to the end strength for FY 2011. The continuation rates, model gain rates, and gain distribution rates are based on five-year historical averages of the civilian gains and losses. The examples presented here reflect data for the entire DoD civilian AW. As mentioned, we have also populated the model with data on subsets of the civilian AW population to reflect the inventory and historical gain and loss data for specific career fields within the AW, specific components of DoD, and career fields within components. With some minor modifications, a manager can use the model to explore alternative assumptions about future workforce turnover or workforce management practices. Customization can be done by modifying some of the model's default gain and loss rates, which are based on the five-year historical averages. Here, we describe the process for making these modifications.

Changing Gain Rates

The model uses two gain rates: the new hire rate and the rate of administrative recategorization into the AW—i.e., the switch-in rate. The new hire rate feeding the model is entered in cell Q26 of the "Base Model—FERS" tab. The switch-in rate is entered in cell Q27 of both the "Base Model—FERS" and "Base Model—CSRS" tabs. The spreadsheet is set up to automatically feed the average rates over the past five years into these cells. However, the user may choose to enter a different rate, as indicated in Figure A.4. For example, one might choose to focus on the actual rates in the most recent year or to play with the rates to identify the one that would be needed to maintain the current workforce.

Figure A.4
Adjusting the FERS New Hire Rate

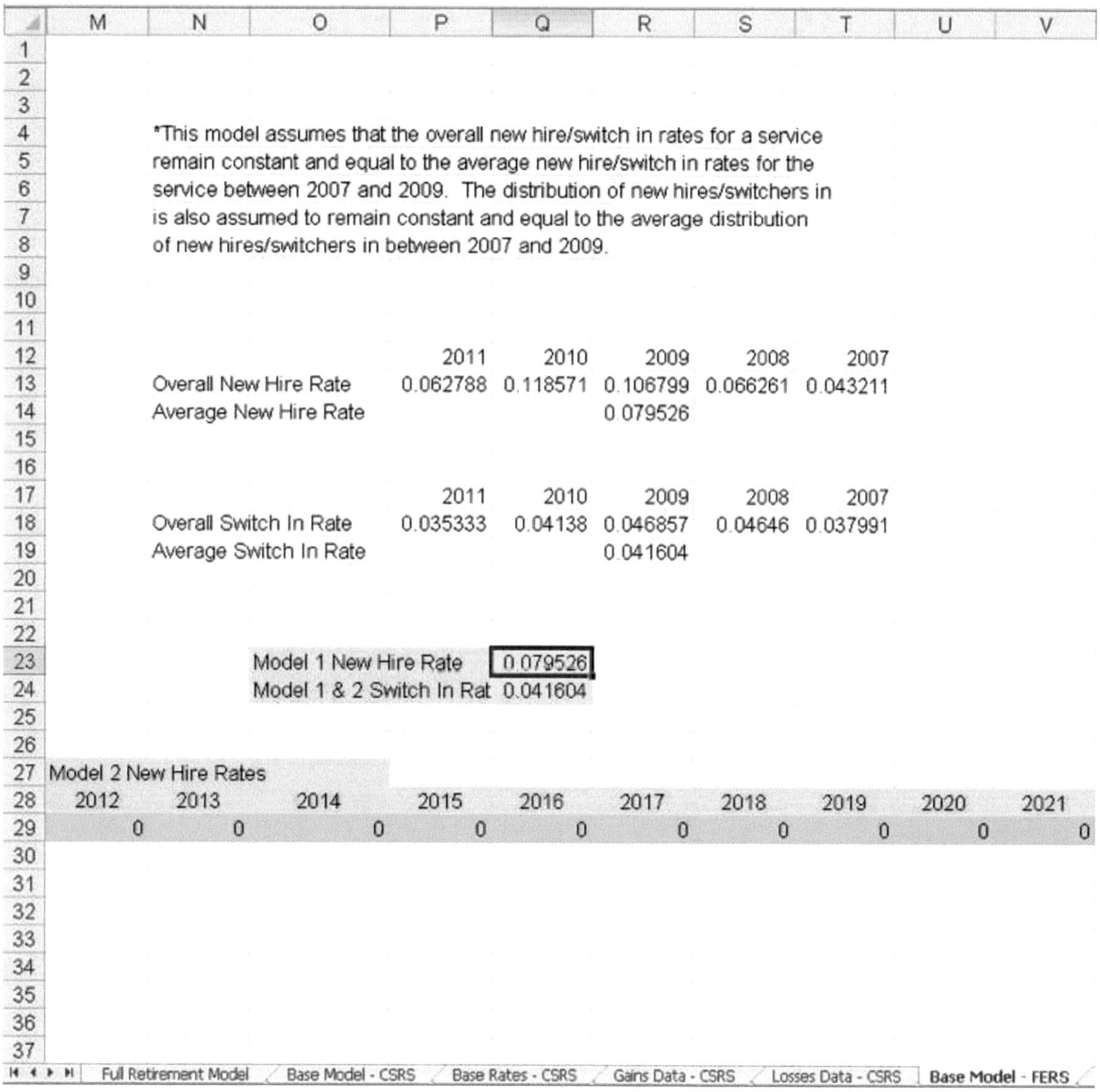

	M	N	O	P	Q	R	S	T	U	V
1										
2										
3										
4		*This model assumes that the overall new hire/switch in rates for a service								
5		remain constant and equal to the average new hire/switch in rates for the								
6		service between 2007 and 2009. The distribution of new hires/switchers in								
7		is also assumed to remain constant and equal to the average distribution								
8		of new hires/switchers in between 2007 and 2009.								
9										
10										
11										
12				2011	2010	2009	2008	2007		
13		Overall New Hire Rate		0.062788	0.118571	0.106799	0.066261	0.043211		
14		Average New Hire Rate				0.079526				
15										
16										
17				2011	2010	2009	2008	2007		
18		Overall Switch In Rate		0.035333	0.04138	0.046857	0.04646	0.037991		
19		Average Switch In Rate				0.041604				
20										
21										
22										
23		Model 1 New Hire Rate			0.079526					
24		Model 1 & 2 Switch In Rat			0.041604					
25										
26										
27	Model 2 New Hire Rates									
28	2012	2013	2014	2015	2016	2017	2018	2019	2020	2021
29	0	0	0	0	0	0	0	0	0	0
30										
31										
32										
33										
34										
35										
36										
37										

Full Retirement Model | Base Model - CSRS | Base Rates - CSRS | Gains Data - CSRS | Losses Data - CSRS | **Base Model - FERS**

RAND RR110-A.4

Changing the Distribution of Gains

This type of change would simulate a shift in recruiting emphasis. For example, a strategy of placing greater emphasis on hiring experienced workers from other agencies or individuals with prior military experience would result in a smaller proportion of gains in the YORE –30 range and greater proportion of new hires with YOREs closer to 0.

The distribution of gains being applied in the model is found in column V of the "Gains Data—FERS" sheet and is based on the average over the last five FYs. To change the distribution of gains, a user would open the "Gains Data—FERS sheet" and scroll down to the gain distribution rates on the lower half of the sheet, then select the YORE cells likely to be affected by the program or policy alternative being simulated and substituting new rates for the ones supplied in the model. Bear in mind that, whenever one cell is changed, offsetting changes must be made so that the distribution rates sum to one.

Changing Continuation Rates

Continuation rates, found in columns D through M on the "Base Rates" sheet, are a key driver of the projection. There is a separate continuation rate for each YOS bin and for each FY. The model assumes that, for each YOS bin, the continuation rate will be 1 minus the average historical separation rate for that YOS bin minus the average historical switch-out rate for that YOS bin. However, the model is set up to allow users to change these separation rates.

This type of change would simulate the effects of increasing or decreasing retention of selected parts of the workforce. For example, paying retention bonuses to workers with selected YOSs would likely increase continuation rates in these years. Likewise, paying voluntary separation incentive pay to the workforce would likely decrease continuation rates, especially for YOS groups in the retirement-eligible range.

Estimating Policy Effects

The model does not have an ability to estimate how much the continuation or gain distribution rates might change as a result of a policy or program change. The user must estimate the direction and magnitude of the effect. One basis for such estimates, if available, would be rates derived from some previous period in which the same or similar policies were in force.[7] By exploring a range of scenarios, the user will understand the range of possible outcomes.

---

[7] In some very sophisticated workforce modeling applications, such as those some services use for military force programming, retention behaviors have been estimated as a function of the alternative income streams for those leaving service and those remaining in service. Such applications readily simulate the retention effects of any policy that can be monetized. However, developing such underlying behavioral models is beyond the scope of work supporting the relatively simple inventory projection model provided here.

Summary Information on AW Gains and Losses

Each year, RAND generates updated summary information on AW gains and losses, for the AW as a whole and for subpopulations of the AW. Table B.1 presents summary information for the overall AW and for select AW career fields. Information on other career fields is available from the authors on request. The table provides information on the total population, number of gains and losses experienced over the FY by type, and some summary ratios that should be of interest to managers. These ratios include the proportion of workforce gains that are new hires (rather than switches in), the proportion of workforce losses that are exits from DoD (rather than switches out), new hires as a proportion of the previous year baseline workforce (hiring rate), and exits from DoD as a proportion of the previous year baseline (exit rate).

Table B.2 presents the same information as in Table 4.1 but includes breakdowns for selected services and DoD agencies. Data for other components is available from the authors on request. Army and DCMA are the only services or agencies that saw declines (–1.35 percent for Army, –0.6 percent for DCMA) in the size of the civilian AW for 2011. Both components had an exit rate of 8 percent in FY 2011, which exceeded the average rate for the AW. Examining the loss rates for the Army in greater detail, we found that, for CSRS employees, loss rates were much higher than in prior years (around 30 percent for those who are retirement eligible and well above 10 percent for those with YORE –1 and –2). This suggests that there may have been an explicit effort to encourage the separation of those who are retirement eligible or close to eligibility and that CSRS employees were more sensitive to these efforts.

Air Force and MDA had a higher-than-average rate of increase in the size of the civilian AW for 2011 (11 percent for AF and 12 percent for MDA). Both components had a higher-than-average new hire rate (9 percent for AF and 17 percent for MDA). DLA and Air Force had a high rate of switching in (roughly 10 percent of the baseline).

Table B.1
Summary Information on AW Gains and Losses

Workforce	FY 2008	2009	2010	2011	Change 2010–2011 (percent)
DoD-wide AW					
Total used for gains and losses	111,495	118,239	132,259	136,066	2.88
Total used for retirement analysis	110,994	117,668	131,585	135,404	2.90
Total with "other" retirement plans	501	571	674	662	−1.78
New hires	7,761	12,216	14,272	8,501	−40.44
Substantive switch in	4,217	4,333	4,259	4,168	−2.14
Administrative switch in	2,267	3,237	5,378	3,524	−34.47
Exits from DoD	6,366	4,751	5,167	7,660	48.25
Substantive switch out	3,318	3,164	2,442	2,370	−2.95
Administrative switch out	5,346	5,127	2,280	2,356	3.33
Total switches in	6,484	7,570	9,637	7,692	−20.18
Total switches out	8,664	8,291	4,722	4,726	0.09
Proportion of gains that are new hires	0.5448	0.6174	0.5969	0.5250	−12.05
Proportion of losses that are exits from DoD	0.4236	0.3643	0.5225	0.6184	18.36
New hires as a proportion of previous year baseline	0.0691	0.1096	0.1207	0.0643	−46.75
Exits from DoD as a proportion of previous year baseline	0.0567	0.0426	0.0437	0.0579	32.53
SPRDE					
Total used for gains and losses	32,403	34,479	36,932	37,786	2.31
Total used for retirement analysis	32,336	34,406	36,847	37,713	2.35
Total with "other" retirement plans	67	73	85	73	−14.12
New hires	1,756	3,066	3,274	1,870	−42.88
Substantive switch in	944	1,011	943	1,068	13.26
Administrative switch in	1,350	1,585	2,628	1,530	−41.78
Exits from DoD	1,404	850	969	1,552	60.17
Substantive switch out	1,104	876	847	740	−12.63
Administrative switch out	1,689	1,860	2,576	1,322	−48.68
Total switches in	2,294	2,596	3,571	2,598	−27.25
Total switches out	2,793	2,736	3,423	2,062	−39.76
Proportion of gains that are new hires	0.4336	0.5415	0.4783	0.4185	−12.50
Proportion of losses that are exits from DoD	0.3345	0.2370	0.2206	0.4294	94.64
New hires as a proportion of previous year baseline	0.0539	0.0946	0.0950	0.0506	−46.68
Exits from DoD as a proportion of previous year baseline	0.0431	0.0262	0.0281	0.0420	49.53
Program Management					
Total used for gains and losses	8,099	8,765	10,262	11,131	8.47
Total used for retirement analysis	8,064	8,724	10,213	11,097	8.66
Total with "other" retirement plans	35	41	49	34	−30.61
New hires	453	917	1,610	985	−38.82
Substantive switch in	847	930	911	881	−3.29
Administrative switch in	879	541	508	487	−4.13
Exits from DoD	456	344	412	576	39.81

Table B.1—Continued

Workforce	FY				Change 2010–2011 (percent)
	2008	2009	2010	2011	
Substantive switch out	686	652	636	503	−20.91
Administrative switch out	851	726	484	405	−16.32
Total switches in	1,726	1,471	1,419	1,368	−3.59
Total switches out	1,537	1,378	1,120	908	−18.93
Proportion of gains that are new hires	0.2079	0.3840	0.5315	0.4186	−21.24
Proportion of losses that are exits from DoD	0.2288	0.1998	0.2689	0.3881	44.33
New hires as a proportion of previous year baseline	0.0572	0.1132	0.1837	0.0960	−47.75
Exits from DoD as a proportion of previous year baseline	0.0576	0.0425	0.0470	0.0561	19.41
Contracting					
Total used for gains and losses	21,730	23,716	25,638	26,065	1.67
Total used for retirement analysis	21,569	23,475	25,322	25,735	1.63
Total with "other" retirement plans	161	241	316	330	4.43
New hires	1,948	2,970	2,809	1,559	−44.50
Substantive switch in	1,329	959	943	947	0.42
Administrative switch in	916	512	442	407	−7.92
Exits from DoD	1,455	1,272	1,395	1,698	21.72
Substantive switch out	650	555	407	466	14.50
Administrative switch out	2,695	628	470	322	−31.49
Total switches in	2,245	1,471	1,385	1,354	−2.24
Total switches out	3,345	1,183	877	788	−10.15
Proportion of gains that are new hires	0.4646	0.6688	0.6698	0.5352	−20.09
Proportion of losses that are exits from DoD	0.3031	0.5181	0.6140	0.6830	11.24
New hires as a proportion of previous year baseline	0.0872	0.1367	0.1184	0.0608	−48.66
Exits from DoD as a proportion of previous year baseline	0.0651	0.0585	0.0588	0.0662	12.60
Audit					
Total used for gains and losses	3,638	3,777	4,124	4,227	2.50
Total used for retirement analysis	3,635	3,774	4,119	4,219	2.43
Total with "other" retirement plans	3	3	5	8	60.00
New hires	434	414	588	339	−42.35
Substantive switch in	464	27	35	33	−05.71
Administrative switch in	180	29	2	0	−100.00
Exits from DoD	215	227	211	226	7.11
Substantive switch out	39	76	64	38	−40.63
Administrative switch out	37	28	3	5	66.67
Total switches in	644	56	37	33	−10.81
Total switches out	76	104	67	43	−35.82
Proportion of gains that are new hires	0.4026	0.8809	0.9408	0.9113	−3.14
Proportion of losses that are exits from DoD	0.7388	0.6858	0.7590	0.8401	10.69
New hires as a proportion of previous year baseline	0.1522	0.1138	0.1557	0.0822	−47.20
Exits from DoD as a proportion of previous year baseline	0.0754	0.0624	0.0559	0.0548	−1.90

Table B.2
Summary Information on AW Gains and Losses, by Service

Workforce	FY 2008	FY 2009	FY 2010	FY 2011	Change 2010–2011 (percent)
DoD-wide AW					
Total used for gains and losses	111,495	118,239	132,259	136,066	2.88
Total used for retirement analysis	110,994	117,668	131,585	135,404	2.90
Total with "other" retirement plans	501	571	674	662	−1.78
New hires	7,761	12,216	14,272	8,501	−40.44
Substantive switch in	4,217	4,333	4,259	4,168	−2.14
Administrative switch in	2,267	3,237	5,378	3,524	−34.47
Exits from DoD	6,366	4,751	5,167	7,660	48.25
Substantive switch out	3,318	3,164	2,442	2,370	−2.95
Administrative switch out	5,346	5,127	2,280	2,356	3.33
Total switches in	6,484	7,570	9,637	7,692	−20.18
Total switches out	8,664	8,291	4,722	4,726	0.09
Proportion of gains that are new hires	0.5448	0.6174	0.5969	0.5250	−12.05
Proportion of losses that are exits from DoD	0.4236	0.3643	0.5225	0.6184	18.36
New hires as a proportion of previous year baseline	0.0691	0.1096	0.1207	0.0643	−46.75
Exits from DoD as a proportion of previous year baseline	0.0567	0.0426	0.0437	0.0579	32.53
Army					
Total used for gains and losses	38,960	38,570	41,991	41,424	−1.35
Total used for retirement analysis	38,693	38,280	41,612	41,063	−1.32
Total with "other" retirement plans	267	290	379	361	−4.75
New hires	2,623	3,448	4,127	2,254	−45.38
Substantive switch in	2,120	1,921	2,089	1,872	−10.39
Administrative switch in	677	744	1,671	1,152	−31.06
Exits from DoD	2,370	1,658	1,682	3,357	99.58
Substantive switch out	2,110	1,828	1,408	1,305	−7.32
Administrative switch out	3,859	3,017	1,376	1,183	−14.03
Total switches in	2,797	2,665	3,760	3,024	−19.57
Total switches out	5,969	4,845	2,784	2,488	−10.63
Proportion of gains that are new hires	0.4839	0.5640	0.5233	0.4271	−18.39
Proportion of losses that are exits from DoD	0.2842	0.2550	0.3766	0.5743	52.50
New hires as a proportion of previous year baseline	0.0626	0.0885	0.1070	0.0537	−49.83
Exits from DoD as a proportion of previous year baseline	0.0566	0.0426	0.0436	0.0799	83.32
Navy					
Total used for gains and losses	37,323	41,184	44,981	46,180	2.67
Total used for retirement analysis	37,265	41,099	44,903	46,123	2.72
Total with "other" retirement plans	58	85	78	57	−26.92
New hires	2,646	4,332	4,383	2,824	−35.57
Substantive switch in	1,284	1,388	1,177	1,263	7.31
Administrative switch in	710	1,460	966	709	−26.61
Exits from DoD	1,774	1,343	1,458	1,920	31.69

Table B.2—Continued

Workforce	FY				Change 2010–2011 (percent)
	2008	2009	2010	2011	
Substantive switch out	1,194	1,095	940	869	−7.55
Administrative switch out	830	881	331	808	144.11
Total switches in	1,994	2,848	2,143	1,972	−7.98
Total switches out	2,024	1,976	1,271	1,677	31.94
Proportion of gains that are new hires	0.5703	0.6033	0.6716	0.5888	−12.33
Proportion of losses that are exits from DoD	0.4671	0.4046	0.5343	0.5338	−0.09
New hires as a proportion of previous year baseline	0.0725	0.1161	0.1064	0.0628	−41.01
Exits from DoD as a proportion of previous year baseline	0.0486	0.0360	0.0354	0.0427	20.57
Air Force					
Total used for gains and losses	16,473	18,475	22,530	24,962	10.79
Total used for retirement analysis	16,420	18,400	22,433	24,861	10.82
Total with "other" retirement plans	53	75	97	101	4.12
New hires	847	2,328	2,781	1,941	−30.21
Substantive switch in	844	986	956	1,142	19.46
Administrative switch in	715	677	2,121	1,145	−46.02
Exits from DoD	952	716	844	1,006	19.19
Substantive switch out	620	642	565	582	3.01
Administrative switch out	273	631	394	208	−47.21
Total switches in	1,559	1,663	3,077	2,287	−25.67
Total switches out	893	1,273	959	790	−17.62
Proportion of gains that are new hires	0.3520	0.5833	0.4747	0.4591	−3.30
Proportion of losses that are exits from DoD	0.5160	0.3600	0.4681	0.5601	19.66
New hires as a proportion of previous year baseline	0.0532	0.1413	0.1505	0.0862	−42.77
Exits from DoD as a proportion of previous year baseline	0.0598	0.0435	0.0457	0.0447	−2.26
Marine Corps					
Total used for gains and losses	1,242	1,505	1,982	2,081	5.00
Total used for retirement analysis	1,238	1,499	1,971	2,069	4.97
Total with "other" retirement plans	4	6	11	12	9.09
New hires	121	254	443	106	−76.07
Substantive switch in	134	138	130	84	−35.39
Administrative switch in	19	43	35	99	182.86
Exits from DoD	69	57	51	111	117.65
Substantive switch out	79	88	67	65	−2.99
Administrative switch out	39	27	13	14	7.69
Total switches in	153	181	165	183	10.91
Total switches out	118	115	80	79	−1.25
Proportion of gains that are new hires	0.4416	0.5839	0.7286	0.3668	−49.66
Proportion of losses that are exits from DoD	0.3690	0.3314	0.3893	0.5842	50.06
New hires as a proportion of previous year baseline	0.1048	0.2045	0.2944	0.0535	−81.83
Exits from DoD as a proportion of previous year baseline	0.0597	0.0459	0.0339	0.0560	65.27

Table B.2—Continued

Workforce	FY 2008	FY 2009	FY 2010	FY 2011	Change 2010–2011 (percent)
DLA					
Total used for gains and losses	3,785	3,971	4,256	4,552	6.96
Total used for retirement analysis	3,781	3,961	4,240	4,523	6.68
Total with "other" retirement plans	4	10	16	29	81.25
New hires	510	360	265	217	−18.11
Substantive switch in	287	399	206	286	38.84
Administrative switch in	13	41	192	115	−40.10
Exits from DoD	168	156	174	167	−4.02
Substantive switch out	141	256	180	136	−24.44
Administrative switch out	186	202	24	19	−20.83
Total switches in	300	440	398	401	0.75
Total switches out	327	458	204	155	−24.02
Proportion of gains that are new hires	0.6296	0.4500	0.3997	0.3511	−12.15
Proportion of losses that are exits from DoD	0.3394	0.2541	0.4603	0.5186	12.67
New hires as a proportion of previous year baseline	0.1470	0.0951	0.0667	0.0510	−23.60
Exits from DoD as a proportion of previous year baseline	0.0484	0.0412	0.0438	0.0392	−10.45
DCMA					
Total used for gains and losses	7,329	7,871	8,441	8,391	−0.59
Total used for retirement analysis	7,229	7,792	8,397	8,335	−0.74
Total with "other" retirement plans	100	79	44	56	27.27
New hires	357	686	810	365	−54.94
Substantive switch in	375	447	460	286	−37.83
Administrative switch in	30	87	84	141	67.86
Exits from DoD	569	444	571	645	12.96
Substantive switch out	151	176	176	171	−2.84
Administrative switch out	77	58	37	26	−29.73
Total switches in	405	534	544	427	−21.51
Total switches out	228	234	213	197	−7.51
Proportion of gains that are new hires	0.4685	0.5623	0.5982	0.4609	−22.96
Proportion of losses that are exits from DoD	0.7139	0.6549	0.7283	0.7660	5.18
New hires as a proportion of previous year baseline	0.0485	0.0936	0.1029	0.0432	−57.98
Exits from DoD as a proportion of previous year baseline	0.0773	0.0606	0.0725	0.0764	05.33
MDA					
Total used for gains and losses	786	922	1,515	1,706	12.61
Total used for retirement analysis	784	921	1,510	1,699	12.52
Total with "other" retirement plans	2	1	5	7	40.00
New hires	75	180	540	250	−53.70
Substantive switch in	130	86	91	64	−29.67
Administrative switch in	6	25	56	15	−73.21
Exits from DoD	32	26	35	58	65.71
Substantive switch out	47	72	54	68	25.93

Table B.2—Continued

Workforce	FY				Change 2010–2011 (percent)
	2008	2009	2010	2011	
Administrative switch out	10	57	5	12	140.00
Total switches in	136	111	147	79	−46.26
Total switches out	57	129	59	80	35.59
Proportion of gains that are new hires	0.3555	0.6186	0.7860	0.7599	−3.33
Proportion of losses that are exits from DoD	0.3596	0.1677	0.3723	0.4203	12.88
New hires as a proportion of previous year baseline	0.1130	0.2290	0.5857	0.1650	−71.82
Exits from DoD as a proportion of previous year baseline	0.0482	0.0331	0.0380	0.0383	0.85

Bibliography

Acquisition Advisory Panel, *Report of the Acquisition Advisory Panel to the Office of Federal Procurement Policy and the United States Congress*, Washington, D.C.: Office of Federal Procurement Policy, 2007.

CBO—*See* Congressional Budget Office.

Chadwick, Stephen Howard, *Defense Acquisition: Overview, Issues, and Options for Congress*, Washington, D.C.: Congressional Research Service, RL34026, June 20, 2007.

Chu, David, and Jeffrey Eanes, *The Trajectory of Personnel Costs in the Department of Defense*, Washington, D.C.: Office of the Under Secretary of Defense for Personnel and Readiness, 2008.

Civil Service Reform Act of 1978 (codified in Part 470 of USC Title 5).

Clark, Charles S., "Army Sets Stage to Slash 8,700 Civilian Jobs," *Government Executive*, August 5, 2011a. As of April 10, 2013:
http://www.govexec.com/story_page.cfm?filepath=/dailyfed/0811/080511cc1.htm&oref=searchbegan

———, "Air Force Announces Civilian Hiring Freeze," *Government Executive*, August 15, 2011b. As of April 10, 2013:
http://www.govexec.com/dailyfed/0811/081511cc1.htm (accessed 12/12/11)

Commission on Army Acquisition and Program Management in Expeditionary Operations, *Urgent Reform Required: Army Expeditionary Contracting*, Gansler Commission report, October 31, 2007. As of April 10, 2013:
http://www.army.mil/docs/Gansler_Commission_Report_Final_071031.pdf

Congressional Budget Office, *A Review of the Department of Defense's National Security Personnel System*, Washington, D.C.: Congress of the United States, November 2008.

Defense Acquisition University, Defense Acquisition Structures and Capabilities Review—Report, June 2007, Pursuant to Section 814, National Defense Authorization Act, Fiscal Year 2006, Defense Acquisition University, June 2007.

Defense Business Board, "Review of the National Security Personnel System," Washington, D.C., FY09-06, July 2009.

Department of Defense Instruction 5000.55, "Reporting Management Information on DoD Military and Civilian Acquisition Personnel and Position," November 1, 1991.

——— 5000.66, "Operation of the Defense Acquisition, Technology, and Logistics Workforce Education, Training, and Career Development Program," December 21, 2005.

DoD—*See* U.S. Department of Defense.

Executive Office of the President, Office of Management and Budget, *The President's Management Agenda*, Fiscal Year 2002.

Fairhall, James, "The Case for the $435 Hammer—Investigation of Pentagon's Procurement," *Washington Monthly*, January 1987.

Farrell, Brenda S., "Performance Management: DOD Is Terminating the National Security Personnel System, but Needs a Strategic Plan to Guide the Design of a New System," letter to the Honorable J. Randy Forbes and the Honorable Madeleine A. Bordallo, GAO-11-524R, April 28, 2011. As of April 10, 2013:
http://www.gao.gov/new.items/d11524r.pdf

Gansler Commission Report—*See* Commission on Army Acquisition and Program Management in Expeditionary Operations.

Garcia, Andrea, Hugo Keyner, Thomas J. Robillard, and Mary Van Mullekom, "The Defense Acquisition Workforce Improvement Act: Five Years Later," *Acquisition Review Quarterly*, Vol. 4, No. 3, 1997, pp. 295–313.

Gates, Susan M., *Shining a Spotlight on the Defense Acquisition Workforce—Again*, Santa Monica, Calif.: RAND Corporation, OP-266-OSD, 2009. April 17, 2013:
http://www.rand.org/pubs/occasional_papers/OP266.html

Gates, Susan M., Christine Eibner, and Edward G. Keating, *Civilian Workforce Planning in the Department of Defense: Different Levels, Different Roles*, Santa Monica, Calif.: RAND Corporation, MG-449-OSD, 2006. As of May 21, 2009:
http://www.rand.org/pubs/monographs/MG449.html

Gates, Susan M., Edward G. Keating, Adria Jewell, Lindsay Daugherty, Bryan Tysinger, and Ralph Masi, *The Defense Acquisition Workforce: An Analysis of Personnel Trends Relevant to Policy, 1993–2006*, Santa Monica, Calif.: RAND Corporation, TR-572-OSD, 2008. As of November 11, 2008:
http://www.rand.org/pubs/technical_reports/TR572.html

Grasso, Valerie B., *Defense Acquisition Workforce: Issues for Congress*, Washington, D.C.: Congressional Research Service, March 11, 1999.

Hanks, Christopher H., Elliot I. Axelband, Shuna Lindsay, Mohammed Rehan Malik, and Brett Steele, *Reexamining Military Acquisition Reform—Are We There Yet?* Santa Monica, Calif.: RAND Corporation, MG-291-A, 2005. As of May 21, 2009:
http://www.rand.org/pubs/monographs/MG291.html

Hedgpeth, Dana, "Pentagon to Expand Its Acquisition Force," *Washington Post*, April 7, 2009. As of May 21, 2009:
http://voices.washingtonpost.com/government-inc/2009/04/pentagon_to_expand_its_acquisi.html?wprss=government-inc

Lardner, Richard, "Army Overhauls Wartime Purchasing," *USA Today*, February 28, 2008. As of May 21, 2009:
http://www.usatoday.com/news/washington/2008-02-28-2650652096_x.htm

Losey, Stephen, "Marine Corps Announces Civilian Hiring Freeze," Federal Times, December 10, 2010. As of April 30, 2013:
http://www.federaltimes.com/article/20101210/DEPARTMENTS01/12100301/Marine-Corps-announces-civilian-hiring-freeze

Lumb, Mark, "Where Defense Acquisition Is Today: A Close Examination of Structures and Capabilities," *Defense AT&L*, January–February 2008, pp. 18–21.

Office of Personnel Management, "FERS—Federal Employees Retirement System Transfer Handbook," *Benefits Officers Center: FERS Election Options,* undated a. As of May 21, 2009:
http://www.opm.gov/retire/pre/election/handbook/h_toc.htm

———, "Retirement FAQs," web page, undated b. As of April 10, 2013:
http://www.opm.gov/retirement-services/retirement-faqs/

———, *FERS—Federal Employees Retirement System Transfer Handbook: A Guide to Making Your Decision*, RI 90-32, 1997. As of February 15, 2013:
http://www.opm.gov/retire/pubs/pamphlets/ri90-3.pdf

———, *Handbook of Occupational Groups and Families*, January 2008. As of May 21, 2009:
http://www.opm.gov/FEDCLASS/GSHBKOCC.pdf

OPM—*See* Office of Personnel Management.

Public Law 108-136, National Defense Authorization Act for Fiscal Year 2004, Nobemver 24, 2003.

Public Law 111-84, National Defense Authorization Act for Fiscal Year 2010, October 28, 2009.

Rostker, Bernard D., *A Call to Revitalize the Engines of Government.* Santa Monica, Calif.: RAND Corporation, OP-240-OSD, 2008. As of May 21, 2009:
http://www.rand.org/pubs/occasional_papers/OP240.html

Shorter, Alexis, Steven R. Burnkrant, Jennifer L. Case, et al., *2002 Summative Evaluation, DoD S&T Reinvention Laboratory Demonstration Program*, U.S. Office of Personnel Management, Personnel Resources & Development Center, 2002.

U.S. Department of Defense, *Quadrennial Defense Review Report*, February 6, 2006a. As of May 21, 2009:
http://www.defenselink.mil/qdr/report/Report20060203.pdf

———, "Acquisition, Technology, and Logistics," *AT&L Human Capital Strategic Plan*, Vol. 1, 2006b.

———, AT&L Human Capital Strategic Plan, Vol. 3, 2007.

———, "DoD and OPM to Review National Security Personnel System," press release, March 16, 2009. As of May 21, 2009:
http://www.defenselink.mil/releases/release.aspx?releaseid=12556

———, The Defense Acquisition Workforce Improvement Strategy: Appendix 1, DoD Strategic Human Capital Plan Update, 2010.

U.S. Department of Defense, Office of the Inspector General, *Human Capital: Report on the DoD Acquisition Workforce Count*, D-2006-073, 2006.

U.S. General Accounting Office, *Acquisition Workforce: Department of Defense's Plans to Address Workforce Size and Structure Challenges*, GAO-02-630, April 2002.

U.S. Government Accountability Office, "High Risk List," web page, undated. As of February 27, 2012:
http://www.gao.gov/highrisk/risks/high_risk.php

———, *High-Risk Series: An Update*, GAO-07-310, January 2007. As of May 22, 2009:
http://www.gao.gov/new.items/d07310.pdf

———, *Defense Acquisitions: Assessment of Selected Weapon Programs*, GAO-08-467-SP, March 2008a.

———, *GAO's High-Risk Areas as of March 2008*, 2008b. As of May 22, 2009:
http://www.gao.gov/docsearch/featured/highrisk_march2008.pdf

———, Department of Defense: Additional Actions and Data Are Needed to Effectively Manage and Oversee DoD's Acquisition Workforce, GAO-09-342, March 2009a.

———, Defense Acquisitions: Assessment of Selected Weapon Programs, GAO-09-326-SP, March 2009b.

———, *Defense Acquisition Workforce: Better Identification, Development and Oversight Needed for Personnel Involved in Acquiring Services*, GAO-11-892, September 2011.

———, *Defense Acquisition Workforce: Improved Processes, Guidance, and Planning Needed to Enhance Use of Workforce Funds*, GAO-12-747R, June 2012.

Vernez, Georges, Albert A. Robbert, Hugh G. Massey, and Kevin Driscoll, *Workforce Planning and Development Processes: A Practical Guide*, Santa Monica, Calif.: RAND Corporation, TR-408-AF, 2007. As of May 21, 2009:
http://www.rand.org/pubs/technical_reports/TR408.html